**THE MENTAL ATHLETE'S
MENTAL POWER DRIVE**

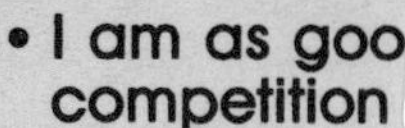

- I am a strong
- I am as goo the competition
- I am relaxed and ready to go
- My body is healthy and well trained
- I trust my body and its strength
- I am successful and I know how to win

"Every top athlete knows that success depends on mental attitudes and concentration almost as much as raw physical ability. Porter and Foster's new book provides insights into the basis of this mental power, along with specific training techniques to help all athletes realize their full potential. I can recommend it highly to anyone who wants to break free of self-imposed limitations and to reach for excellence."

Joan Ullyot, M.D.
Marathoner and author of
Women's Running and *New Women's Running*

"Most coaches know that negative thinking doesn't get the job done but they are not sure how to implement total positive thinking. This book shows you how!"

Ron Finley
Head Coach, 1984 U.S. Olympic Greco-Roman Wrestling Team

THE MENTAL ATHLETE:

Inner Training for Peak Performance

Kay Porter, Ph.D., and Judy Foster

Foreword by Joe Henderson

BALLANTINE BOOKS • NEW YORK

Library of Congress Catalog Card Number: 85-71679

ISBN 0-345-34174-0

This edition published by arrangement with William C. Brown, Publishers

Interior illustrations by Marilyn Belwood

Illustrations on page 136 adapted from a photograph by Jack Mitchell

Manufactured in the United States of America

First Ballantine Books Edition: June 1987

18 17 16 15 14 13 12 11 10 9

Dedication

This training is dedicated to you, the athlete—the beginner, the weekend mover, the young and aspiring, the elite, and the coach. With your wisdom, your inspiration, your support, this training evolved and matured. Thank you.

Man is what he believes.

Anton Chekhov

CONTENTS

Foreword

You are what you think. And in sports, that can be either a blessing or a curse, depending on the quality of that thinking.

I was both blessed and cursed as a young athlete with an active imagination. In the years before many people ran or anyone practiced formal sports psychology, I caught a vision of myself as a successful distance runner. I wasn't built along the classic long and lean lines of a miler, and lacked coaching help and training facilities. But because I thought I could run a mile fast, I did—winning four state high school championships at that distance.

Psychology worked for me then. It worked against me soon afterward, when I began to think that my potential was limitless. I thought if I aimed high enough and worked hard enough, no one could beat me.

Then I lost to runners with equal will to win and more talent for doing so. The losses were crushing, because the expectations were so overblown. I started thinking of myself as a loser, and stopped competing for fear of losing any more.

The problem worked itself out only during a long period of readjusting to my self-image and redefining winning in more personal terms. Even after the thoughts improved, this episode left me with deep respect for the powers of the athlete's mind.

You are what you think. In sports, that can be a problem or an opportunity, depending on how you choose to use the body from the neck up.

Lack of motivation and effort aren't problems for most athletes. They're more often troubled by wanting too much and working too hard for it. Their ambitions stifle their abilities. They compete with their mental brakes on, fearing failure while not allowing themselves to succeed.

The opportunities for success in sports may not be unlimited, but they still are vast. Every athlete has untapped potential, and yet very few athletes tap a source of immediate and dramatic improvement: mental training.

"Training" implies specific, planned, preparation for an upcoming event. Physical training is standard practice in all sports. Mental training should be but isn't.

Athletes can move ahead mentally the same way they do physically: through training that accentuates positive factors and eliminates negative forces, and by preparing the intellect, emotions, and spirit as carefully as the heart, lungs and legs.

This ideal balance rarely exists. Athletes who put their physical preparations under a microscope give mental training no more than a passing glance. They can't be blamed for this oversight. Little guidance has been given on how, exactly, to train mentally.

Writing on sports psychology generally runs toward the poles. At one extreme are the cliches and platitudes that have supported generations of coaches in their peptalks. These center on the "you can do anything if you want it bad enough" theme. If it were only that easy. . . .

At the other extreme are books by psychologists who smother readers with research data and technical jargon. An athlete without an advanced degree in this field can't translate the theoretical material into practical terms.

Thankfully, Kay Porter and Judy Foster don't fit into either category. They follow a middle course between the extremes. The Mental Athlete is simply without being simplistic, and technically solid without forgetting that most readers are athletes, not Ph.D. candidates in psychology.

Porter and Foster offer their advice in the best tradition of physical training books. They give both the "whys" and the "hows," combining theories with practices.

The writing reflects the twin interests of the authors, who counsel athletes professionally as well as compete themselves. Their mental training plans blend the expertise of the psychologist with the concerns of the athlete to produce specific self-help programs.

Porter and Foster involve athletes as co-authors of these programs right from chapter 1, because they realize that the final solutions to problems must come from inside oneself. Readers of this book are certain to find their own answers much faster than I found mine.

Joe Henderson, West Coast Editor of Runner's World

Preface

It all began because we are athletes and because we are women. Each time we competed or trained for competition, certain issues arose. They were mental issues, women's issues and athletic issues. Was it unfeminine to be a good athlete? Was it acceptable to take time to train? Why did we perform poorly after making a mistake or losing? What do we do with the frustration when we are injured and have to rest? Why did we doubt ourselves and our abilities?

Nowhere were we able to find satisfactory answers or an effective plan of attack that would help us move as athletes to a higher level of performance and achievement. There was nothing "wrong" with our performance—we were not "head cases", we simply wished to achieve on a higher level, to reach beyond our present, known potential.

We began to seek, to watch, to explore, to question. We spent hours with coaches, personal growth advocates and counselors, elite athletes, high achievers, and dreamers. We taught, we observed, we learned, and we taught some more. After two years, we have developed this comprehensive mental training for the general as well as elite athlete and coach. We feel extremely good about our program and this book. It is a book not so much from the head but from the heart. It is a training—it takes time and it will give results which go beyond your athletic world. It will change your reality.

Judy Foster

Now I know how the Oscar winners feel as I try to remember to thank all the people who have inspired me, encouraged me, taught me, and stimulated my mind, body and spirit. The list is long, beginning with the first glimmering of my personal growth at Esalen in 1969, continuing through the 70s in death and dying seminars with Elisabeth Kubler-Ross and Stephen and Ondrea Levine, and into the 80s in Therapeutic Touch, healing and personal effectiveness seminars from Gary Koyen & Associates. My growth has been a continuous flow of life, death, and rebirth. After years spent in computers, aging, death and dying, and personal transformation, in 1980 I happily began my third professional incarnation in the field of sports psychology.

A colleague recently mentioned a book that describes the astrological destiny of the United States. The astrology chart of the United States apparently has two primary and singular major personality characteristics. The overall persona of the United States is controlled and determined by the sports and consciousness movements. These two seemingly diverse interests and passions of the American people will, in my opinion, result in a tremendous cultural explosion and the enrichment of American personal and professional potential.

When my friend told me of this book and its descriptions, I felt an electricity surge through my body. I felt that Judy and I would become two of the pioneers of this movement. The power and excitement I have experienced since then has sometimes been overwhelming. Each day we have worked on this book, I have had a feeling of euphoria, excitement, clarity, and purpose. Never before have I experienced such feelings for such a long period of time. As described in chapter 5 on visualization, my body has been constantly filled with feelings and emotions of being "right on" and in perfect synch with Judy and our environment.

At a recent workshop Judy and I taught with Bob Hackman,

a sports nutritionist, I personally experienced for the first time a peak performance of such magnitude that I was euphoric for hours. As I facilitated the group one evening, an immense energy, concentration, and focus poured from me and through me. I was merely the vehicle through which the experience and energy flowed. I "knew" everything to say, do, or be—without conscious thought. As I "came down" from the experience, my first thought was, "My God, what have we done here?" I had the perfect "flow experience." Writing this book has been much the same. It has flowed through us without effort. It is my hope and dream that all people and athletes will sometime experience this feeling of perfect union of body, mind, spirit and environment—complete and total unity.

Let it be easy. Let the knowledge, the inner knowing, and your intuition guide you simply with purpose, clarity, and perfection throughout your life. Learn to let go and to let it be. Learn to be centered and to flow.

Kay Porter, Ph.D.

Acknowledgments

We would like to acknowledge and thank:

Dr. Gary Koyen for his ideas, knowledge, and support. The concepts discussed in chapter 1 especially reflect lecture material from the Koyen and Associates seminars on Personal Effectiveness. These seminars helped us solidify our thinking and inspired us to apply many ideas and concepts such as accountability, responsibility, and belief systems to sports psychology and mental training.

The University of Oregon Athletic Department and the coaching staff who were open and trusting enough to let us work with their athletes and teams.

The Athletics West/Nike and unattached athletes who so willingly agreed to interviews with us. Their information provided us with valuable insights into the psychological processes of competition and the elite athlete.

Joe Henderson, who was an inspiration, model, and mentor, and who believed in us and our work even when we questioned ourselves.

Joan Ullyot whose book, *Women's Running*, and personal friendship provided the inspiration to begin.

Marilyn Belwood for her phenomenal drawings and illustrations and hours of research.

Bob Sevene, whose support, trust, and friendship encouraged us when we most needed it.

Steve Eiring and Paul Brothers for their help and expertise.

Tom Jordan, who gave us our first assignment.

Our mates, children, parents, and friends who provided us with unlimited opportunities and who have put up with every conceivable emotion and inconvenience in the pursuit of this goal, the research and writing of this book.

All others who have participated in our lives on all levels, who have taught us, led us, followed us and otherwise given to us the tools we have used.

THE MENTAL ATHLETE

CHAPTER ONE

Introduction to Mental Training and Its Basic Assumptions

For this is the great secret, which was known to all educated men in our day: we create the world around us, daily new....

M.Z. Bradley

What do Carl Lewis, Joan Benoit, Greg Louganis, and Mary Lou Retton have in common? Assorted Olympic medals, world and American records, and most importantly tremendous mental skills that enhance their athletic performance and put them at the top of the field in their events. The program of mental training comprehensively defined in this book will, if used with dedication and discipline, help you reach the top of your peak athletic performance Before the 1984 Olympics, we had

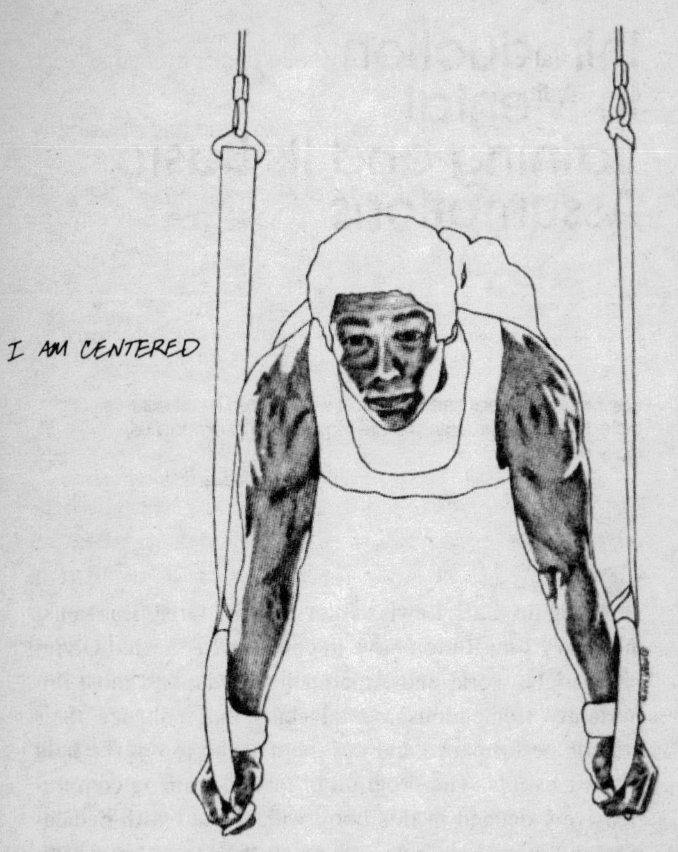
I AM CENTERED

an opportunity to interview a number of elite athletes about what they do in the way of mental preparation, that is, mental training, for their events and we found the following common skills.

- total belief in themselves and their physical abilities
- absolute and total concentration and focus during competition
- visualization of their performance for days or weeks before the event
- analyzing any losses in order to improve performance and techniques or strategy
- ability to let go of defeats easily and look forward to new challenges in future competitions
- never seeing themselves as losers, even after losing a competition or two

And when we explain to elite athletes what methods and techniques we teach in mental training, many respond, "I've been doing that for years; it just sort of came naturally." Indeed, they have intuitively learned and practiced these techniques on their own. The good news is that anyone can learn these strategies and employ them in any athletic performance.

The whole idea of mental training is to focus on the positive aspects of mental performance, physical abilities, and preparation skills. The stigma of being a "headcase" is gone. The old medical model focused on what was "wrong" with us. This program focuses on what is "right" and how to expand it to make it work for you and improve your performance. You don't have to be sick to get better.

The basic assumption of a mental training program is that the pictures in our minds have real power and that we create our own reality with our mental images, that is, how we "see" ourselves and our abilities, whether positively or negatively. These images affect our performance now and in the future. For example, if you "see" yourself as a slow and rather awkward person, you will manifest this physically when you attempt an athletic event. If, on the other hand, you train yourself to "see" yourself a winner and competent athlete, this too will manifest itself in your performance.

Research is now telling us that the pictures in our minds, our visualizations (and we all have visualizations), create the climate and atmosphere of our world. We can and do create either positive or negative images for ourselves as people and as athletes. As we create these images, we are putting forth an "intent" of what will happen to us. Think for a minute, about the last time you were around someone who was angry. You could "feel" their negative energy from across the room. Think now of the last time you were with someone who was excited, happy, and full of energy. Remember how their energy made you feel and how it affected your attitude and responses. If we go into an athletic performance or competition feeling scared, unsure of ourselves, and uptight, our co-athletes or competitors will be able to feel this negative energy and it will show in our performance.

If we can feel calm and confident, we can create a positive atmosphere. By expecting the best, we create and set up a "positive intent" that good things will happen, that we will succeed.

By creating positive intent, you become a dreamer. You day-dream, you think of what you want and what you believe is possible—or maybe even impossible. You imagine what kind of difference achieving a particular goal will make in your life, your work, your athletic performance and abilities. You "dream the impossible dream," and by dreaming it you make it possible.

What exactly is mental training for peak athletic performance? It is the learning, practicing and application of mental and psychological skills through

- short- and long-term goal setting
- changing negative thought patterns and perceptions into positive thought and belief systems (reframing)
- writing positive self-statements (affirmations) about and in support of your athletic performance
- progressive relaxation
- visualization and imagery in your event
- concentration and focusing
- coping mentally with injury and pain

It is a training program exactly like your physical training program. This means that for it to work best, you must practice it everyday or at least every other day. It requires discipline and your whole being supporting your athletic goals and dreams.

Though the very elite athlete seems intuitively to set up his or her own individual mental program and may feel he or she does not need a comprehensive program, there are at least five groups of athletes whom we have found could successfully benefit from this mental training:

- any talented athlete who has yet to achieve his or her potential
- female athletes who need to learn to be more aggressive and competitive
- elite athletes when they are injured
- elite athletes when they wish to improve their concentration and focus
- all of us who participate in sports and wish to improve and reach our peak performance

The response of athletes to sports psychology and mental training ranges from, "Hey, don't fool around with my head!" to "Sounds great! I'll try anything to be better at what I am doing. It's worth a try to see what I can learn." And, of course, every response in between. The smart athlete of the eighties is one who is willing to work with every new idea to improve his or her performance. Many coaches and athletes maintain that peak performance is 90 percent mental. All of us, from the elite athlete to the average, can learn by using this simple program and practicing mental skills as diligently as we practice our sports.

Self-Accountability/Self-Responsibility

How often have you as an athlete lost and blamed others, or blamed yourself for your poor performance and perhaps the loss of the entire game? Is this attitude positive and does it work for you, or does it help to keep you stuck at your present performance level? Do we learn from our experiences or are they always someone else's fault? The bottom line is that we and we alone are responsible for the level of our performance. We may not be responsible if a fan throws a tin can and hits us in the head, but we are responsible for our reaction to that event. We are responsible for our level of readiness and for our positive or negative frame of mind as we prepare to perform. We choose to learn from a less than perfect performance or event and go forward, using it to our advantage, or we choose to become upset and tense and are defeated by our attitude. We are totally free to see ourselves as important, competent, talented, and unique or as incompetent, unworthy, untalented and second best.

All of these choices are made in our minds, colored and dictated by our self-concept and personal support. Many times, accepting this concept takes maturity and trust—trust in the process of living and trust in ourself as a competent athlete and person, trust in our "gut feeling." Take a moment to look at your own level of trust. What do you trust most about your athletic performance? What do you trust least about your performance? What do you think your coach or teammates trust most about you? What do they trust least about you? You may wish to write these thoughts down to clarify your level of self-trust and to discover what, if any, improvements could be made.

It is easier to make choices and create inner trust if we feel directed—if we have goals and the desire to head toward them and if we are willing to be accountable for the choices we make and their consequences. With this new found responsibility, we must reassess the way we approach competition and life.

Do you as an athlete view competition or important workouts as a threat, as a challenge or do you enter them for the love of the game? Think of the last big event you participated in that meant a lot to you. When the big play came to you or when the outcome depended totally on you, did you pull it off or did you lose your concentration and choke? If you did succeed, what was your feeling? Relief? Joy? Elation? If you did not succeed, were you filled with self-hate, strong, sharp anger with yourself for days or weeks? Or did you feel disappointed and dissatisfied for a few hours and then went on with life? If you enter your event feeling threatened, when you win you only experience relief; when you lose, you hate yourself and blame yourself or others for months or years. If you view competition as a challenge, you experience joy if you win and strong anger when you lose. Challenge often works as a strong motivator for many athletes and can be a fairly successful strategy. If you participate simply for the love of the game and win, you savor that victory. You feel ecstasy and great enthusiasm. And when you lose, you may be disappointed but you learn from your mistakes and go on knowing that you are not the loser, you have merely lost and will win again. The loss does not destroy your self image, your self-esteem, or your belief in your abilities.

The most successful athletes often perform between challenge and love of the game. They love their sport, they have fun doing it, and they are spurred by challenge. They understand that the attitude they bring to their performance is their choice and that it will either help them win or defeat them.

If we have taken the time to prepare mentally for our performance, realizing it is fully our choice; if we have formed our goals and feel directed and in control—we will succeed many times far beyond our expectations. We will win even if only within ourselves and we will experience the feeling of accomplishment that accompanies our peak performance.

Belief Systems

The basic assumptions of personal growth advocates are that we are not our programming. We are not our ego, we are not our personal past, we are not our acts, we are not our failures or our successes. Then what are we? Good question. We are what and who we think we are. If we see ourselves as losers, as victims, we will surely make ourselves so. If we believe we are competent, powerful, and winners, this is our reality. Our beliefs become self-perpetuating and self-confirming. How we think and believe determines our experience by confirming our beliefs and self concepts and creating our reality. We can change these belief patterns so they work for us and change our reality to a positive and supportive system. It is possible, but it takes time. It means becoming aware of which beliefs limit us and risking changing what may be a lifelong habit. For example, below are some common belief systems that limit many athletes in their sport and in their lives in general:

- I have to earn respect.
- I must compete to please my Dad.
- I have to earn love.
- No pain no gain.
- It's not OK to have fun.
- It's not feminine to be an outstanding athlete.
- It's selfish to take time for myself and my training.
- I'm too slow, too dumb, too fat, too tall, too short (etc).
- It's not feminine to beat the boys.
- Being an outstanding athlete makes me acceptable to my peers.

Mental Trainer #1: Beyond your Limits

List some of your limiting beliefs about your athletic performance that you feel may be hindering your performance. Think about this. For all of us, it is extremely difficult to "see" our habits, to see what it is that may be holding us back from reaching our highest level of performance.

My limiting beliefs:

These limiting beliefs keep us stuck in the mud of our minds. They take away our power and feelings of competence and confidence. By "power" we mean a feeling of competency and well-being, not brute strength. It is a feeling generated by our inner voice and mind, a true sense of "knowing." Go inside yourself for a moment and ask yourself:

How do I feel when I feel powerless?

How do I feel when I am in my power, when I feel powerful?

What do I do to be in my power, to feel powerful?

How does it feel, sound, and look when I am in my power?

Listen to yourself as you continue these awareness questions. Be in touch with how connected or disconnected you are at this point with your personal mental process and how it guides your experience and reality.

Three ways I strip myself of my power in my sport:

Three things I do to help myself keep my power in my sport:

The most significant mental change I could make to reach a higher level of athletic performance would be:

This book is about finding your mental awareness, noticing what you do with it, and learning to make it work for you in every aspect of your life. To grow and learn in both athletics and in life, you must be willing to do the following:

- take risks
- feel what's going on for you, especially in competition
- be in the present moment and let go of the past
- breathe when you are tense or scared
- have fun and enjoy
- trust yourself and the process
- participate 100 per cent without fear of failing or making a fool of yourself

Winning is as hard or as easy as you make it. The choice is yours. In an interview with Judi Brown-King, the 1984 Olympic Silver medalist in the 400m hurdles, we asked her about the importance of mental training and its impact on her performance.

"Since I started running, I've always considered myself a mental runner. If I didn't believe I could do it, I wouldn't have a good race. You're describing me when you say 'mental training.' I started doing mental training when I first began running, but I started doing the mental preparation before I realized what I was doing. Especially the night before, I would break every world record there was in my images. The early morning, before I run, is when I really get into mental preparations. I imagine every single thing that could happen to alter the race—it's windy, it's raining, I hit the hurdle, I feel the "hump" between hurdle five and seven. That's the hump for me, the most difficult part of the race, and I know the feeling, so in the race I am ready for it. I've mentally prepared myself for it and I know how to react to it appropriately.

"For instance, I tell myself, 'so and so in the race got an excellent start . . . don't panic . . .', and I adjust to that situation. I more or less know all the runners in the race and how they run so my images are very accurate. I've always been that way in life, preparing myself for any outcome. In all my tests through school, I'd figure out what the teacher stressed as important and learn that. I found myself to be very perceptive as to what someone perceived to be important.

"When I start visualizing a race, the first thing I feel is that adrenalin surge. If you were to hook my heart up to an EKG and I started visualizing, my heart rate would probably go from low to a very high rate. I can imagine and visualize everything, even with my eyes open. Five minutes before a race is a runner's nightmare. Anything can happen. No matter how physically and mentally prepared you are, you can totally lose everything in the last five minuts. If you are distracted, you have to be able to pull yourself back on track mentally and refocus and concentrate. Even being strong minded, you have to be able to turn negative situations into positives. The mental games runners play are amazing. For instance, when I started racing, one runner whose times were slightly better than mine, came over before a race and sat directly in front of me so I could see her. Her "game" was to get me to focus on her instead of preparing myself for my race. It takes a strong mind to shut out a predicament such as that and still be successful.

"Our event isn't that full of games, but there are some events like the 100, 200, and 400 meters that are mentally vicious. I had a choice of a second event and I chose the 800 because the 400 was just too full of games. The majority of us in the intermediates hurdles are good friends. When we are running a heat, others will say, "come on, you can do it!" We cheer each other on. I like the rapport of my event.

"As I mentioned before, in the last five minutes before the race, I prepare myself. When the official says, 'Runners, take your mark,' I think about driving out of the blocks, getting out well, because if I have an excellent first hurdle, I'm going to have an excellent race. If I have just a good start, I'll have a good race. Likewise, if I have a bad start, I'll have a race of adjustments. The main thing I think about is, 'get out . . . get out!!' Then when the starter says, "set", I just think about the gun and wait for the sound to react to.

"Even my negative experiences have become positive in the long run. I'm basically a positive thinking person. In the difficult parts of my race, I turn it off (mentally) the pain threshold. I concentrate on the mechanics of movement. I'm thinking about snapping that lead leg down, instead of thinking 'I'm tired,' or possibly, 'I'm behind' . . . I concentrate on staying relaxed by saying, 'stay relaxed.' If I hit a hurdle, I say, 'it's OK . . . let's make up the momentum you have lost.' I tell myself, 'OK, you're still in good shape, up with the top three runners, let's try and get up in second or first so there are no more mishaps.' Things like that. I give myself continuous pep-talks."

One of Judi's most telling statements is, "The five

minutes before the race is a runner's nightmare." And indeed, it can be for the athlete whose emotions are out of control and whose self-talk is negative. For one who has practiced mental control, it can be a time of solidity, mental toughness, and centeredness. The daily practice of mental training techniques can turn those five minutes into a pleasant interlude, a precursor to fulfilling a lifetime dream and goal.

The last 100 or 200 meters of a race again calls for mental tenacity. "What were you thinking during that last 100 meters of the Olympic finals?" we asked Judi. "I was telling myself, 'I've worked hard for this. Listen, I've given up too much to give up here! At least try for a medal!' I was running for my sacrifices. I began catching people. Nawal (the gold medalist) was too far ahead to catch. I ran negative splits (running the second half of the race faster than the first). All in all, I was satisfied.

"If I get down, distracted, or whatever, I make a decision to just turn it off. I don't let myself dwell on a situation or let it get to me. I didn't enjoy the Olympics too much. I had bad starts; I got lane 8 when I should have had lane 6, but somehow it wasn't given to me. I just put these situations on the shelf and turned it off mentally. I wouldn't let any 'bad breaks' get to me."

It is this style of conscious decision making that an athlete can learn to use. It can become a habit like anything else. The athlete chooses, like Scarlet O'Hara, to "worry about it tomorrow." This strategy can help the athlete focus on his or her event and block out everything else. The mental state is one of acceptance, letting go, and returning internal focus to the event. Judi Brown-King is an excellent role model in terms of attitude and mental preparation. "I am basically a positive person and turn negative things around into a positive situation for me. I refuse to let things pull me down." Certainly she is a positive role model athletically. She is a smooth and rhythmic runner and has beauty and grace going over the hurdles. Even in practice doing her drills, she has style and grace. Her inner strength and peace are reflected both in her attitude and her athletic performance. Brown-King is an excellent person for aspiring young athletes to emulate.

CHAPTER TWO

Goal Setting

Goals are a preview of future events and experiences in your life.

Mark Victor Hansen

The basis of any mental training is a goal or goals. Goal setting is the clearest way of establishing a consistent program for training and competition in your sport. It is also a powerful form of direction and motivation for both individual athletes and teams as a whole. The effects of a goal-setting system are cumulative. As you achieve your first goals, you will become more certain of what you want from yourself and your sport and just how to accomplish it. Learning to set short-term, intermediate, and long-term goals is one of the most powerful tools any athlete can use to increase measurably the level of his or

I AM QUICK AND STRONG

her performance. Your goals become the framework that guides your training and your competitions. Your goals, whatever they may be, and the desire to achieve them, are the motivation that pushes you through the rain and snow, through pain and injuries, and through the times when you may feel stuck at a certain level or plateau.

A goal is anything we wish for, dream about, or choose to achieve. It can be easy, hard, possible, or seemingly impossible. Goals are not something we make judgments about; they are simply something that we choose to pursue and achieve. Whatever your goals, they must be specific to you. They must be yours; not your parents', not your mate's, not your best friends', or even your coach's. They must be what you want. "Goals must be for each individual, not for someone else. You must remember that you only have control over your own behavior. As much as you might like to change the behavior of others, you cannot. You must keep in mind that the only behavior that you can change is your own" (Harris & Harris, *An Athlete's Guide to Sports Psychology: Mental Skills for Physical People, 1983*).

General Goals

It is important that your goals "feel" realistic to you and yet are challenging. We set goals to improve our level of performance, and none of us knows exactly what our limits are. If we say our goal is simply to improve or to do our best, we leave too much room for confusion and lack of risk and motivation. Evaluating our present level of performance and analyzing your past history will help you form goals that are realistic for you and that challenge and push you beyond what you may think is possible. Goals are sometimes the only way we can measure our progress. Therefore, it is important that our goals are measurable and specific. As you progress in your sport and begin to achieve your goals, step by step, you will begin to measure your success in terms of your progress rather than in terms of wins and losses. If you have structured your goals in a positive way, each time you lose or win will mean that you have achieved some goal.

Stop for a moment and think of what you wished to accomplish when you began your sport. What was it that intrigued you about it? Why did you choose your specific sport and what did you wish to achieve? Become aware of where you are now in this sport. How has your ability changed and what do you want from yourself and your sport right now? Where are you going? Where do you want to go?

As the answers begin to come to you, write them down. Make a list of all the things you wished for in the beginning and all the things you hope to achieve now and in the future. Just allow them to come randomly and write them below. Do not give yourself time to worry about achieving these goals or about failing or succeeding. Simply put them down if they are important to you without analyzing them further at this point. At the same time, begin to imagine what kind of difference the achievement of these goals will make in your performance or competition. What will it look like and feel like to you to accomplish these goals?

Mental Trainer #2:
Sport Goals

Goals I wish to Obtain in My Sport:

Short-Term, Intermediate, and Long-Term Goals

Once you have this list, begin to order and categorize your goals according to importance and time frame. Which are the most important to you? Which can be reached this month, and which may take a year? It is important to work with two to three goals at a time. Pick three for this month, three for the next six months, and three for the next year. To avoid feeling overwhelmed, you may wish to number them and place an S for short-term, an I for intermediate, and an L for long-term next to the goal number. Short-term goals are usually those aimed at a specific workout or competition taking place within the next two weeks or even the next three days. Short-term goals tend to be very clear and specific such as: "I want to maintain an eight minute pace throughout my entire five-mile run tomorrow," or "I want to rush the net each time I serve, being aggressive and ready throughout the entire match in my doubles competition next weekend."

Intermediate goals may also be specific as well as broad and less well defined. They are usually goals you wish to reach within the next six months and may need several steps to achieve. Many times, the steps to our intermediate and long-range goals become our short-term goals. For example, we are working with a college sprinter whose long-term goal (end of the season) is to run in the NCAA championships. His intermediate goal is to make the Pac Ten team (mid-season). And his short term or immediate goal is to run a PR (personal record) in his first outdoor competition in two weeks.

If you try to work with more than two or three goals at one time or do not set your priorities, you may never know what you want, when you want it, or how to get it. After prioritizing from your list above, pick the three most important short-term, intermediate, and long-term goals and write them below. Now is when you should spend time analyzing exactly what you mean by each goal. What does it "look" like to you? Define your goals in writing as clearly as you can so you are aware of exactly what they mean to you, and how it will feel to work for them and achieve them. If you notice that you have some resistance to a certain goal as you write it down and define it, simply acknowledge the feeling and let go of it for the moment. In the next chapter we will deal with the negative feelings and fears that sometimes come up when we seriously contemplate reaching for a goal.

Mental Trainer #3: Goaltending
30-Day Goals *Definition*
6-Month Goals *Definition*
1-Year Goals *Definition*

It is also important to realize that no goal is etched in stone. Our goals change as time changes, as our physical abilities change, and as our personal circumstances change. You will find that as you let go of one or two goals for whatever reasons, one or two new ones will quickly come to take their place. This is a natural sequence of events in your growth as an athlete.

Steps for Achievement/Mini-Goals

For many of us, figuring out how to achieve any given goal seems overwhelming, and we sometimes resist starting at all and avoid working toward any goal. This feeling of frustration and confusion can be easily handled by taking the time to think of and write down at least three "steps" you can take, one at a time, toward achieving each goal. These "steps" are actually mini-goals and serve to simplify our way to the larger goal, reducing the stress we feel when choosing to reach for a goal.

For example, you are a downhill skier. The giant slalom is your event, and you wish to improve your time by 45 seconds by the end of the season. This looks to you like a chance to move up in the individual standings, resulting in your having more credibility as an athlete. How can you reach this goal? Forty-five seconds is a lot of time, and much depends on the layout of the gates, the drop of the course, the snow and weather conditions. What small steps can you take in just about any situation that would improve your time and your speed? Perhaps you could take the gates a little higher than you usually do. Maybe if you didn't allow your uphill arm to fall behind, you could pick up a few extra seconds. Maybe if you leaned into the hill a slight bit more your speed would increase.

Goal: To take 45 seconds off my giant slalom time by end of the season (five months). This will help me feel more credible as an athlete and improve my self-image.

Step 1 Prepare for and approach gates at a higher angle.

Step 2 Keep both hands in front of my shoulders at all times.

Step 3 Research and analyze all new waxes and bases for all conditions at least one week before competition.

Maybe you are a middle-distance runner beginning the indoor season. If you are tall, you know the uncomfortable feeling you get when running on the boards around the turns, which are banked and tight. You feel as if you might fall over or lose control of your form and rhythm, so you slow down when entering the turn and feel your entire body tighten. This costs you time and more energy to catch up once you enter the straightaway. Your ultimate goal for the indoor season is to do well enough to make the nationals, but this means you would have to take at least three seconds off your previous best time.

Goal: To make nationals this year for indoor track. This means taking at least three seconds off my best time. Making the nationals would help me feel as if all the time and energy I have put into my running is finally paying off.

Step 1 Use the turns . . . don't be afraid of the turns and slow down and lose time. Attack the turns and be in control.

Step 2 Know that I am as good and as fast as anyone else on the track and relax into the race.

Step 3 Lengthen my stride and push harder in the backstretch instead of worrying about going too fast and not having enough left for the finish.

For the next 30 days your short-term goal is to learn to attack the turns and overcome your insecurity. Every time you work out or compete for this next month, your concentration is focused on how you approach the turns and use them for your benefit so that you are in control of your whole race and subsequently reduce your time.

Below, list your long-range goals and define them as you have above and then list three mini-goals or steps that will help you in the long term to achieve these goals.

Mental Trainer #4: Step by Step to Success

Goal #1:

Define

Step 1:

Step 2:

Step 3:

Goal #2:

Define

Step 1:

Step 2:

Step 3:

Goal #3:

Define

Step 1:

Step 2:

Step 3:

This exercise can, of course, be used for all your goals to help you clarify and achieve each goal. Once you become used to this process, any hesitation or lack of confidence in reaching for a goal will lessen and you will succeed.

As we stated in chapter 1, it is important to understand and accept that we are not our acts, we are not our failures and we also are not our successes. Becoming aware that the process of goal setting gives us a sense of direction and control over what we do and where we go in our lives requires an understanding that being successful or failing occasionally has nothing to do with our personal self-worth as an athlete or a human being. Few of us are successful in everything we attempt. Being willing to risk, to reach, to move beyond beliefs and fears that may be preventing us from realizing our peak performance is the purpose and the ultimate goal.

CHAPTER THREE

Positive Self-Statements

It has been said many times that the only difference between the best performance and the worst performance is the variation in our self-talk and our self-thoughts and attitudes.

Dorothy and Bette Harris

When we were born, our spirits were free of belief systems. We had no concept of fear, love, rejection, competence, acceptance, hate, and so on. We were taught. We were taught to be gentle, to love, to know what can hurt us physically, to risk, and to limit ourselves. For the most part, we were unconscious of this learning process. Over the years our parents, teachers, peers, neighbors, churches, bosses, and mates told us

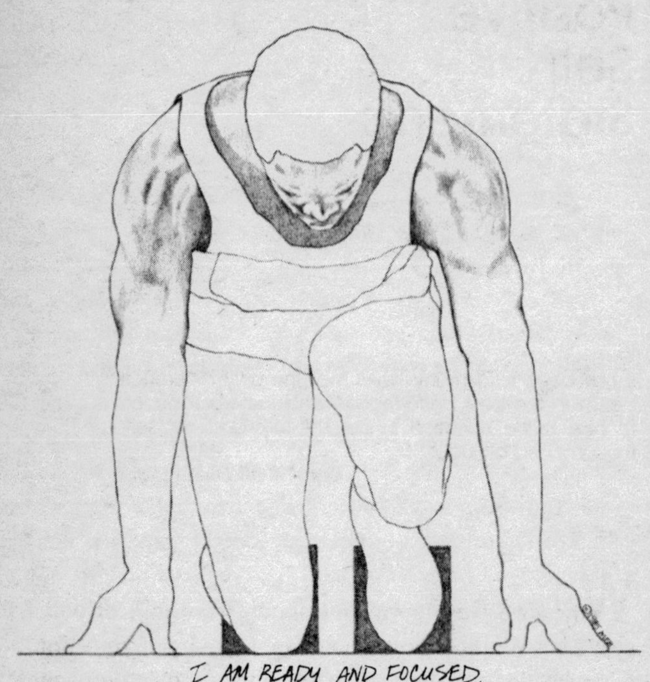

I AM READY AND FOCUSED.

such things as "Don't cross the street or you'll get hurt"; "Be nice to your sister/brother"; "You're too dumb... too little... too fat... too short"; "You can't do that"; "Girls don't do that sort of thing"; "Being an athlete makes you a man"; "Your body is bad and dirty"; "Love is better than war"; "Feelings make you weak"; "Don't cry"; "Be nice to everyone"; "Life is to suffer through"; "Every rainbow has a pot of gold at the end"; "Be afraid of strangers"; "Winning is everything"; and on and on. Sound familiar?

First, we should all know that whatever our belief systems, they were learned and can be unlearned. Secondly, we should become aware of which of our beliefs work for us, support our spirit and usefulness in the world, and which ones limit us, defeat us, and cause us pain. It makes a lot of sense to be careful when crossing the street or to be wary of strangers. But does it work for us to believe that women are too weak to participate in some sports or that it is unfeminine to be better than the boys? Does it work for us to believe that if you are not interested in sports or not very good at them that you are less a man? Does it work for us to believe that we can't? Does it ever work for us to believe that if we don't win we are failures?

Think back to chapter 1 and the personal attitudes that athletes such as Mary Decker, Greg Louganis, and Carl Lewis have in common. Below are three of the six:

- total belief in themselves and their physical abilities

- analyzing any losses in order to improve performance and techniques or strategy
- never seeing themselves as losers, even after losing a competition or two

How did they get there? Some were always there, they intuitively knew they were good, competent, and strong and that it was perfectly acceptable for them to reach for any goal they chose. And some taught themselves because they found it worked, little by little, to believe in themselves. The latter may be the major reason you are reading this book. We think it is one of the most important reasons we wrote this book. How we hold ourselves in our hearts and minds is how we perform in life in general. What we believe to be true about ourselves determines our successes, our failures, our ability to risk, our strength to handle any situation, and ultimately how we treat ourselves and those we deal with in life.

"The athletes' message is clear. The difference between best performances and worst performances lies within their thoughts" (Orlick, *In Pursuit of Excellence*, 1980). Think of your last two or three competitions or workouts. Were they good? Did you achieve a new PR? Or did you fall short of your goal? As you were performing and afterward for the next 24 hours, what was going on in your head? What, if anything, were you saying to yourself? Think of what you say to yourself on a day-to-day basis. Does it sound something like this: "Oh, you stupid idiot . . . how could you do such a dumb thing?";

or "Man, you'll never beat that person . . . just look at how strong he/she is"; or "No way can I perform well in this weather or when all these people are watching me."

In the middle of one of our workshops, a young woman raised her hand and said, "Every time I show up at the track for a competition I am so tired, I have no energy, no motivation. It's like I just don't want to be there, like I'm bored or something. And so I start to get on my case about feeling that way and then everything tightens up and I usually don't do very well." She was saying things to herself such as, "Oh come on . . . you can't win if you're always so lazy!" and "What makes you think you can even run when you are bored and acting so stupid?"

Keeping in mind that your thoughts control and sometimes dictate your emotions, take a minute to think about your self-talk, your self-concept, and then begin the worksheet below:

Mental Trainer #5: My Self-Talk

What I am saying to myself before a workout:

Positive

Negative
What am I saying to myself before a competition: *Positive*
Negative
What I am saying to myself after a competition: *Positive*

Negative

Now, as you begin to have a clearer picture of what you say to yourself, read the positive things again and relate them to your performance. Notice how they helped you to stay focused, to push ahead, to try harder, or simply to feel good about your performance and therefore yourself. Now read the negative thoughts. Notice if there were more negative thoughts than positive, when they occurred, and what happened to your focus, your form, and your performance when you listened to them and kept them in your conscious mind. How did they distract, limit, or defeat you?

Positive self-statements (affirmations) are a powerful weapon we can all use to combat the destructive self-beliefs and talk we confront from time to time during workouts and, more specifically, during competitions. For most of us there is a fleeting period of nervousness or self-doubt. Those are the times to use an affirmation to change your focus and energy. Affirmations will short-circuit the negative talk. An affirmation is a positive self-statement that usually is not true at the time but supports the way you wish to view yourself and your abilities or a goal you wish to achieve during this specific workout or competition.

Affirmations are always positive, present tense, and personal. They are positive because the subconscious does not take in negatives, and they are positive because that is the whole point—to change the doubt or destructive thought into one that supports and enriches your confidence, self-concept, and performance. Affirmations are present tense because it is very important to be in the here and now. They are something you want to believe is true right now. And an affirmation is always personal. As we have said, we have control only over ourselves, no one else. By using positive self-statements, you are working on changing your personal belief systems, your destructive self-concepts.

Suppose that some of your negative self-talk looks and feels like this: "I don't know why I'm competing today. I am not ready and I'm tired"; or "Oh no, he's here today. I never can beat him"; or "The last time I really blew it. I messed up the whole competition"; or "What if I fall or come in last and everyone sees me?" What we want to do is to change these thoughts so they support us and help us to know that we are in control. As affirmations, the above thoughts would look like this: "Well, here I am again and I am ready and feeling good and strong. I have practiced well and I am prepared." And "I knew he'd be here and I am ready for him. I am just as good an athlete as he is. I am more than capable of beating him." And "Boy, I really learned a lot from the last time and I now know exactly what to do. I am confident and competent." And "I am in control all the way and I enjoy the crowd and their enthusiasm. I am performing well and taking energy from the great crowd."

Affirmations are "I am" statements. They are the reverse of your negative, limiting self-talk. You may not feel that they are true at this moment. When you were "learning" all the limiting self-beliefs they also were not true but because you bought the idea—someone else's idea—you went about the business of making these beliefs part of your reality. Since we know we create our own reality, we now can create a positive, unlimited, supportive self-reality. It's a matter of buying a new set of beliefs, ones that are positive and self-nurturing.

Take a look at your negative thoughts written above. How can you make these positive, present tense, and personal?

Mental Trainer #6: Transformers

Negative thought #1.

Positive affirmation: I am

Negative thought #2.
Positive affirmation: I am
Negative thought #3.
Positive affirmation: I am

The harder it is to form a positive statement from one of your negative beliefs, the better it will be for you and the more important it is to change it to a positive self-statement. By this we mean that if you write: "I am strong and confident and capable of beating anyone at this competition," and it feels strange in the pit of your stomach or you laugh and shake your head, or if it is difficult to write down and say to yourself, then it is perfect for you. It is an important one for you. Try these for example:

- I believe in my own ability as an athlete.
- I have a positive mental attitude and self-image.
- I do excellent mental preparation for my event.
- I believe in myself.

- The more I believe in myself, the more I am able to employ the talent I possess.
- I am strong and powerful.
- I am in control and focused.
- I love to compete and push myself, reaching for my goals.
- Physical exercise is good for me and I enjoy it.
- I am prepared and relaxed.
- I enjoy performing before a crowd and appreciate their support.
- I am a capable and competent athlete.

Once you have changed all your negative thoughts into positive self-statements, write your old, negative statements on a piece of paper. Now physically get rid of them. You may want to burn the paper or bury it. Maybe you could put it in a bottle and send it out to sea or perhaps give it to your dog to eat. Whatever you do, release yourself from these thoughts and bring your focus back to the positive statements and beliefs that are now becoming a part of your reality.

Find your list of goals from chapter 2. Read them again and think of how you are going to achieve each of them and what you wish to experience at that point. Remember our sprinter whose short-term goal was to run a PR in his first outdoor meet? We asked him what he was afraid of in this meet and exactly what he would have to do and feel in order to reach his goal. He said that he knew some of the other sprinters who would be there and one of them was a medalist in the Olympics. Also, he felt his starts were not very good. He hated coming out of the blocks. He wanted to feel in control and light and strong throughout the whole race. These were his affirmations in support of himself and his goal:

- I am prepared and in control.
- I am as good as any runner on this track today.
- I am powerful and light, using long, easy strides.
- I am focused and relaxed.
- I run well all the way with power and confidence.
- I enjoy coming out of the blocks and feel balanced and quick.
- I am having fun!

He not only PR'ed but beat everyone to the rousing applause of the crowd. He remembered repeating some of these statements just before getting into the blocks at a time when he was feeling a little unsure. He also remembered feeling relaxed through the whole race and knowing he could do what he asked himself to do.

Go back to your goals and pick one from each group —one short-term, one intermediate, and one long-term . . . and write them on the next worksheet. Then write at least three affirmations in support of each goal. For example:

1. Short-term goal: I want to stay on the balance beam throughout my entire routine. I want to feel in control and light and make it all the way through.

Affirmations: 1. I am balanced and in control.
2. I am performing perfectly throughout my entire routine.
3. I am light and controlled staying on the beam through my whole routine.

Mental Trainer #7: Goaling Forward
Short-Term Goal: *Affirmations:*
Intermediate Goal: *Affirmations:*
Long-Term Goal: *Affirmations:*

You should go through this process each time you make a goal for yourself. Because positive self-statements support what you wish to achieve as well as help you change your negative belief systems to positive, they cause you to put out a positive "intent" to the world around you. Your control of and gradual belief in this positive intent is what begins to change your reality. The more you support yourself and your athletic endeavors, the more the world around you will support you, and achieving your goals will become easier and easier.

Read over the affirmations you just wrote. Are you using can or will in your sentences? Have you written, "I will always be in control and focused"? or "I can stay on the beam without falling"? The use of words such as can and will puts your intent too far in the future. It causes your mind to believe that it will always have time and gives it an excuse for not believing in your abilities now. This limits your ability to change your reality; it is always out there somewhere and you remain only partially in control.

Though you may review your list of goals only once a week or so, it is important to read your affirmations at least twice a day. The best times to read them are before you turn your light out at night and in the morning before you put your feet on the floor to start your day. These are times when you are relaxed and your mind is uncluttered with demands or cares. When we are the most relaxed, our subconscious is the most open to receiving new ideas and beliefs. The deeper we are able to receive these positive self-statements, the sooner they become reality.

Once you are familiar with your affirmations, there are many times in your daily athletic life when they come in very handy. Anytime you feel tired or sore in a competition, or if self-doubt begins to creep into your thoughts as you perform, reach inside for these positive statements and they will help you maintain focus, confidence, and control. They will help you believe you can push yourself further, reach higher, run longer or faster, move beyond any self-imposed limitations. Though it is important to acknowledge pain or fatigue, it is ultimately important to go beyond, to release it, and focus on the positive in order to reach your peak performance.

I AM A RELAXED AND CONFIDENT PLAYER.

CHAPTER FOUR

Relaxing and Nourishing the Whole Person

The process of relaxation produces a sense of mind-body integration, a state of mind that sports psychologists have noted as characteristic of superathletes.

Charles Garfield

For many of us, the hardest task in athletics and in life in general is to know how and when to relax, to know who and what helps us feel good about ourselves and our world and therefore promotes a state of relaxation and well-being. The second most difficult task is achieving a state of balance—balance between training and rest; balance between work and play; balance between seriousness and spontaneity; balance between relaxation and readiness. We get caught up in what we "have to do" or "should do," or "should be." This imbalance costs a lot.

People and Activities That Promote Relaxation

We know that the more relaxed and at ease we are, the more we feel in balance, and the better our performance, whether in sport, at work/school, in our relationships, or in our creative endeavors. But how do we achieve this balance? How do we find and maintain this kind of harmony within ourselves so we can achieve our personal peak performance? One step is to become aware of the things we do, the people we know, and the places that give us joy, peace, support, learning, and growth. All of us seem to be very good at "knowing" all the things, situations, people, and so on that make us feel insecure, angry, or frustrated with ourselves. Seldom do we take the time to be honest and self-nurturing enough to really connect with all the things that add to our lives and that balance the more negative things to which we seem so clearly attached. To be effective and successful athletes, we should know who and what promotes our being centered, our confidence, our relaxation and our having fun.

Mental Training #8: What I Love to Do

List all the things you love to do. List the things that give you happiness and confidence, the things you may not allow yourself to do because they make you feel so good that something inside tells you it's not OK to be so happy.

List all the people you enjoy being with, sharing with and giving to. These are the people who put you at ease. Though you may see each other infrequently, still it feels natural and easy each time you get together. They are the people who support and care about you in their hearts and toward whom you feel the same.

With these lists in mind, complete the drawing below, including both the people and activities or things from the above lists. Fill in the circles closest to you with those people or things you consider to be the closest, most important, or most nourishing to you. Those you feel least strongly about will go in the circles furthest from you. Think clearly and deeply about each one. What does this person really mean to you and what does he or she give or receive from you and your relationship that helps build the peace and happiness within yourself? Ask the same questions of the activities or things you enjoy. Suppose one of the most important things to you is backpacking along your favorite river every summer no matter what. What is it about that spot, that river, that physical activity that nourishes you so much that you relax and find peace and contentment there more than anywhere else? What is it you find that pushes you to go there without fail every year?

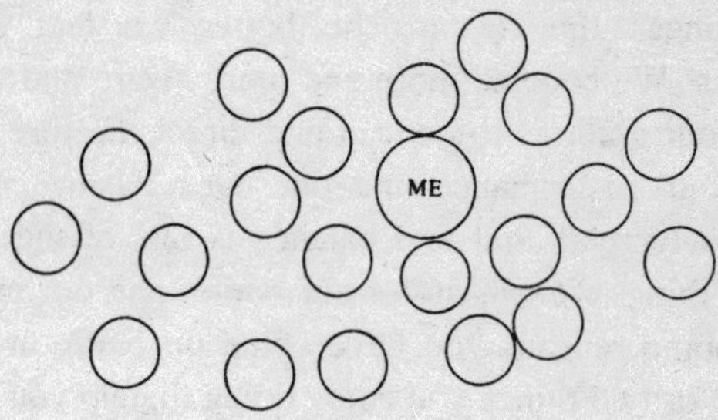

Are you surprised by some of the things or people you included? Are you amazed at how good it feels to connect with that thing or person that brings joy and relaxation into your life?

The next step is to give yourself permission to, at least once a week, enjoy being with one of these nourishing people or do one of those things that delights you. This means making and taking the time to give yourself a relaxing, stress-reducing, self-supporting gift once a week regardless of how busy you are. Once a week spend some time with someone or do something that nurtures your relaxation and gives you a sense of peace.

The more positive things we do for ourselves—the more we allow ourselves to enjoy the company of those who support us for the people we are—the fewer negative things will we do against ourselves. The more positive changes that occur, the better we feel about ourselves. We become more and more aware and confident of our abilities to control and direct the forces affecting our performance and our lives. Using certain exercises to relax and find balance is one of the more positive things we can do for our bodies and our minds. If, for some reason, you have come up blank or with only one or two things you enjoy doing to help you relax and feel good, we have several suggestions. To begin to understand what it takes for you to relax, not only in life but for major workouts and competitions, give yourself permission to try one or two of the methods we have found most beneficial to the athletes we have worked with as well as for ourselves: breathing, meditation, massage, floatation, and progressive relaxation.

Breathing

Breathe! Sounds funny, right? Everyone breathes, especially athletes. Not everyone, however, uses breathing to the best advantage especially in athletics and, most importantly, to relax and renew energy before, during and after competition. Correct breathing is one of the most valuable techniques for focusing, calming, and energizing that an athlete can learn. "As we free our breath through diaphragmatic breathing, we relax our emotions and let go of our body tensions" (Hendricks & Carlson, *The Centered Athlete*, 1982). Diaphragmatic, or belly, breathing is the easiest form of breathing to learn. The belly rises and falls as the lungs are fully inflated, and the diaphragm stays loose and flexible. Breathing is rhythmic and deep. Because most of us are thoracic (chest) breathers, it takes some practice to learn to fill the belly area completely with each breath, easily inhaling and exhaling without forcing the abdominal muscles to expand and contract. Diaphragmatic breathing increases the amount of oxygen taken into the bloodstream and therefore increases the amount available to the muscles. A greater amount of air is exchanged when we breath deeply, causing our breathing rhythm to slow and become more steady. This, in turn, calms the nerves and steadies the emotions, bringing about relaxation and a sense of control.

"Proper diaphragmatic breathing involves the entire torso. It is useful to envision this breathing pattern as a three-step process. First, the diaphragm moves downward, creating a vacuum in the chest cavity that draws air into the lower portions of the lungs. Next, the middle part of the lungs begins to inflate, and the abdominal area expands . . . from just below the rib cage to just above the navel. Finally, the chest itself expands, filling the upper portion of the lungs." (Garfield, *Peak Performance*, 1984)

When exhaling, follow the same steps outlined above; emptying your abdominal area first, then the middle part of the lungs, and finally the chest and upper lungs. Each time you exhale, let go of old energy, tiredness, and tightness. Become empty and ready to receive new, clean energy and relaxation. Inhale, feeling new, vital strength flowing in . . . exhale, releasing old tiredness and tenseness.

When we are afraid, nervous, or worried, we tend to restrict our breathing and hold it tightly, high in our chest or even in our throats. This cuts off even normal oxygenation and causes us to feel fatigue and to lose physical coordination and mental concentration. Becoming aware of our breathing, focusing on its rhythm and depth, will enhance our energy, our control, our concentration, and ultimately our performance.

Meditation

Meditation is a clearing and quieting of the mind. Thoughts are focused in one quiet direction, and all other distractions, chatter, and ideas are released. Meditation initiates a general decrease in your body's metabolism, your heart and breathing rate, and an overall decline in your body's need to utilize oxygen. Therefore, reserve using meditation as a form of relaxation for times when you do not expect to be immediately physically active. Meditation is an excellent way to relax the night before competition if you find sleep or a sense of peace difficult to achieve. Meditation helps diminish muscular tension in the major muscle groups and helps you to restore body balance before and after intense physical activity.

Find a quiet time and place, a place where you are comfortable both physically and mentally, and sit or lie in a relaxed posture that supports your body. Close your eyes and think of a few words or sounds that take little effort to say. Breathing deeply and quietly, begin saying these words or sounds in rhythm over and over, gearing them to the ebb and flow of your breathing. Focus on only the words or sounds until your mind becomes empty of all else. Be aware momentarily of the physical relaxation as it slowly moves over you and you begin to disconnect with your body, staying focused only on the sounds and their rhythm. Continue your meditation for at least fifteen minutes, allowing nothing to distract you or enter your mind but the sounds and words you are repeating. Let it be. "So it is with the greatest efforts in sports; they come when the mind is as still as a glass lake" (Gallwey, *The Inner Game of Tennis*, 1974).

When you feel fully at peace and as if you are "finished," begin to reconnect with your body. Slowly and gently move your head to the right and then to the left and to the center. Breathing quietly, open your eyes and your mind to the space you are occupying.

If you meditate before bed as a form of relaxation and sleep preparation, you may find that you fall asleep easily long before 15 or so minutes go by. This is the purpose of your meditation. If you find that your mind is wandering, continue to work at keeping your focus on the sounds or words. Do not worry. With practice, you will learn to stay focused and to use this form of relaxation anywhere when you feel it necessary to quiet and clear your mind in order to focus your attention where you want it.

We like to think of T'ai Chi Ch'uan as a form of physical meditation. The body is taught and allowed to find a quiet, rhythmic movement containing strength, balance, concentration of mind and body, and patience. Each movement has a meaning and a purpose. Your breathing should be synchronized with the rhythm of your total movement.

For example: stand with your right foot slightly ahead of and apart from your left foot, finding a comfortable balance and control. Find a spot or focal point straight ahead and hold your visual attention there. With all body parts aligned over your center (two inches below the navel), knees slightly bent, and your eyes fixed on one point ahead of you, move forward onto your right foot leaving your left foot entirely on the floor. Then rock back with your weight onto your left foot leaving your right foot completely on the floor. As you move forward, exhale—inhaling as you move back to your left foot. With elbows at your sides and forearms parallel to the ground, palms down, slowly "push" away from your body as you move forward to your right foot, rotate your palms until they are facing up, and slowly, as if scooping, "pull" them toward you as you rock back on your left foot bringing new energy to your body. Rotate your hands again, palms away from your body, and "push" as you exhale and move forward onto your right foot; rotate, palms up and "pull" toward yourself as you inhale and rock to your left foot. Repeat this movement over and over, establishing a rhythm and emptying your mind and body of all other thoughts or physical distractions. Become one with the movement and rhythm of your breathing. Allow yourself to relax into it and to become part of it, without thought or need to tense or stiffen. Remember to keep your shoulders relaxed and to trust yourself. Occasionally focus on your center and feel the energy radiating to all parts of your body. To really learn T'ai Chi, one usually needs to find a good teacher and take a class. It is difficult to learn from books alone.

Massage

For any athlete, there are few things that give more relief from tension and minor physical soreness or tightness than a good, deep massage. Almost any town, city, or metropolis has at least one trained and licensed masseur or masseuse who is qualified to touch, rub, knead, and otherwise manipulate your muscles to stimulate circulation and cause relaxation of tenseness and soreness. You can usually ask for a full-body or half-body massage. We recommend a full body massage since it covers all major muscle groups as well as the feet, face, neck and head. It brings about more complete and overall relaxation and stress reduction.

If you, as an athlete, are seriously active every day, you would benefit from having a massage at least once a week. You will find your body has more energy, is ready and balanced, and so performs at a higher level if you aren't carrying around areas of tightness and stress. A consistent massage program will also help you remain injury free by loosening, warming and relaxing all muscles and reducing your tension level.

Floatation

Though sensory deprivation tanks have been used since the 1930s, only recently have they been available to the general public and athletes. We know them today as floatation tanks. When we use them for relaxation, we "float." Present-day tanks look something like a plastic egg. They are six feet wide and approximately nine feet long and are filled with more than a hundred pounds of epsom salts and about twelve inches of water. It is impossible for your body to sink. The water temperature is

93.5°F or about 30°C, which is skin temperature. Most tanks are fitted with an underwater sound system so you can listen to music or audio tapes of any kind. Some tanks also have video screens, and many athletes watch technique tapes while they float.

Plan on about one and a half hours if you are going to float. You must take a shower before entering the tank as well as after you have floated. The usual time allotment is one hour, though some places offer a half hour float time. You may wear a bathing suit or nothing. You may leave the hatch-door open if you fear claustrophobia, though it is more effective if you close the door and float in the dark. (The door is never locked and can be easily opened from inside.) Of the athletes we have sent for a float who worried about claustrophobia, all decided to close the door and none had any problem with the space or the air.

Once in the tank, relax! Your head will not sink, though your ears are usually under water. Rest your body and your mind for a few minutes. You may wish to close your eyes or leave them open. Open your thoughts to anything that comes. Let go and relax as you float effortlessly and weightlessly. There are no sounds, no feelings, no smells—only darkness. Let yourself become an empty blackboard, empty and unused. Slowly become aware of any stimuli such as spots or colors before your eyes or a sense of turning or lightness. Notice these things, enjoy them, let them go and remain empty and at peace.

If you are training for a specific event or competition,

floating is the perfect time to say your affirmations and begin your visualization and mental rehearsal (chap. 5). If you have brought a guided visualization tape with you, this is also the time to have it played on the underwater sound system. Allow yourself to experience everything as you go through your entire visualization. Because you are so totally relaxed, your affirmations and the visualization will move further than usual into your subconscious. Your mind is more receptive and the subconscious more vulnerable to what you want it to learn. This means that the neural patterns you are developing will be stronger.

When you leave the tank and shower and enter your day again, you will notice a renewed energy along with a feeling of total relaxation. A float twice a month is what we recommend to maintain balance and center yourself. This will help you be more deeply relaxed and create a deeper level of visualization.

Progressive Relaxation

Progressive relaxation is another form of physical relaxation that, in turn, relaxes the mind. It focuses on the major muscle groups of the body and involves tensing and relaxing each of these groups one at a time. This is the most common form of relaxation used before visualizing, as it effectively produces deep relaxation of both the mind and the body as well as establishes a deep, calm breathing pattern and awareness. Though floating in a tank will actually put you on a deeper level of relaxation, it takes a special place and usually costs money. Progressive relaxation can be done anywhere and any time you have a few minutes of quiet.

There are basically two forms of progressive relaxation: the long, total body process and the short, immediate form that can be used after you are thoroughly familiar with the long form.

LONG FORM

If possible, find a quiet, comfortable place to sit or lie. You will need about ten to fifteen minutes. Sit comfortably in the chair with both feet flat on the floor and relax with your hands at ease in your lap and your back against the back of the chair. If you are lying on the floor, rest with your arms at your sides, legs fully extended, and your back flat. Begin to relax, center your body parts and clear your mind. "Centering" means aligning all body parts so they are well supported and equally connected with each other. Imagining your center of gravity and power located two inches below your navel will make you feel calm and relaxed and will enhance your sense of balance and strength. Progressive relaxation is started on your dominant side. If you are right handed, start with the right arm. If you are left handed, begin by tensing the left arm. Close your eyes and focus on your breathing. Inhale deeply into your diaphragm . . . hold it for a moment . . . and exhale from your belly up to your chest. Inhale . . . hold . . . exhale.

Empty your mind, allowing any random thoughts to pass through. Feel your body and mind letting go. Inhale . . . hold it . . . exhale.

Beginning with the dominant hand, forearm, and bicep, make a fist (not too tight), hold it feeling the tension in your arm, and let it go, completely relaxing. Make a fist of your other hand . . . hold it . . . let go. Moving to your head, tense your forehead, your nose, and your jaw, squeezing your eyebrows together . . . hold . . . and let the tension go, feeling it float away from your consciousness. Breathe. Hunch your shoulders up around your ears . . . hold . . . let them go and feel a sense of relaxation begin to flow downward, over your belly, past your hips, down your legs, and into the floor. Allow yourself to let go on a deeper and deeper level with each relaxation. Slowly begin to roll your head to the right . . . to the front . . . and to the left. Pause. Move slowly to the front . . . and to the right . . . back to the front . . . and relax with your head comfortably resting on your neck. Breathe and move your awareness to your abdominal area. Slowly contract your abdominal muscles, pulling them back toward your spine . . . hold . . . and release with a sigh. Now to the dominant leg. Push our heel into the floor . . . hold feeling the tightness in your thigh . . . let go. Point your toes ahead of you, feeling your calf tightening . . . hold . . . release. Move slowly to the other leg. Push your heel into the floor . . . hold . . . release. Point your toes ahead of you . . . hold . . . release, feeling all tension and connection with your body leaving your awareness. Breathe deeply . . . exhale. Inhale new energy and vitality; exhale tiredness and tension.

SHORT FORM

This form of relaxation is but one version and can also be used before a visualization once you have mastered the ability to totally relax yourself physically in a short period of time. It can be done anywhere. It may take as little as two to three minutes or up to seven minutes depending on your desires and the time available to you. Take a quiet moment, close your eyes, and center on your breathing. Breathe in deeply and hold it for a moment, letting go and allowing your mind and body to relax and become empty and peaceful. Inhale . . . hold . . . exhale.

Move your awareness inside and notice if there are any areas of tightness or places where you feel sore or uncomfortable. Begin on your most dominant side and check in with each muscle group. If you feel some tension or soreness, acknowledge it, send it some energy and peace, and let it go. Move your awareness from side to side and from head to foot, acknowledging any tension or tightness and any pain or discomfort, sending care and energy and letting go. Return to your breathing anytime you find it difficult to let go or move beyond some pain or tension. Re-center yourself and then go back to that area and let it go, allowing it to relax and become soft.

When you feel fully relaxed and centered, you are ready to begin your visualization, or you may begin to reconnect with your physical space by moving your fingers and toes and slowly opening your eyes. This short technique for relaxing is ideal for just before and after competition. We also recommend it in any stress-inducing situation such as before an exam, at work when you feel overwhelmed, or when a relationship is stressful and there is a need for calm, controlled communication.

Because our lives, both athletically and in general, tend to place more stress on us from time to time than we feel capable of coping with, any form of relaxation is vital to our mental and physical health and well being. Whether you simply choose to go to a movie with your best friend, take a walk, spend twenty minutes doing T'ai Chi, or float in a tank, nourishing yourself both in mind and body will bring balance and focus to your athletic performance. It will bring a high level of control to your life and help you reach any peak performance you choose.

CHAPTER FIVE

Visualization and Mental Imagery

What you see is what you get.

Flip Wilson

The pictures we "see" in our mind's eye, the inner "pictures" we feel or hear through our subconscious and conscious, have real and lasting power. They dictate and determine our reality. They help us to risk making changes, understand how better to approach a problem or deal with difficulty, and create and clarify our thoughts. They also limit our performance, our self-concept, our ability to change, learn and produce in our world. How we view ourselves—our abilities, our acceptability, our intelligence, our worth—ultimately

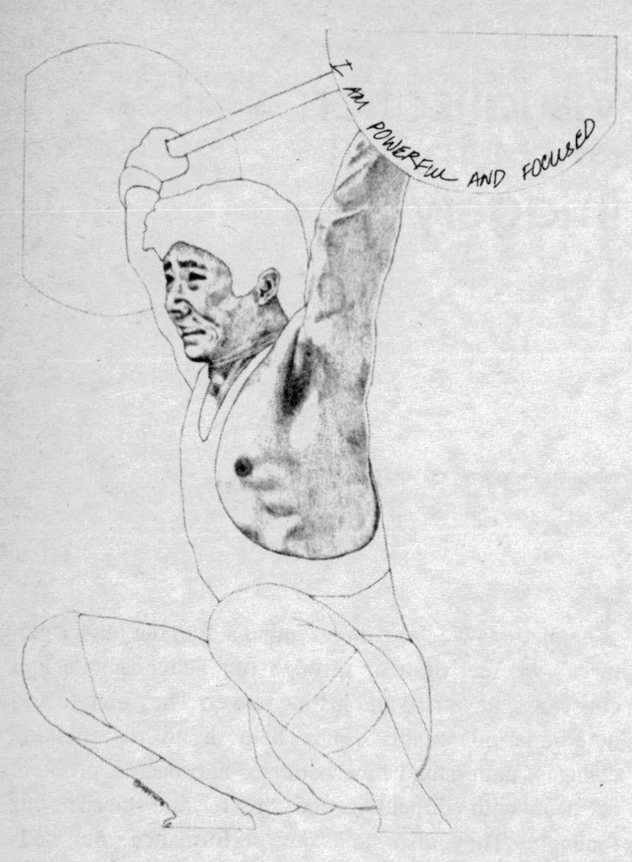
I AM POWERFUL AND FOCUSED

determines who we become, what we do, and what we have—our reality.

Some people "see" within their mind. This means they can actually see a picture. Some see this picture from within, meaning that they see their performance as if they are in their own body and looking out. They see the track in front of them as they run, or the balance beam before them as they mount and begin their routine. Others see from without, in other words, they watch themselves perform. To be able to do both would be optimum; however, few of us can initially. You can learn to see it both ways if you are willing to work at it and give yourself time.

One week after the 1984 Olympics, Mary Decker was interviewed about her fall in the 3000 Meter race. She was asked if she had visualized the race. Had she "seen" herself running in the Olympics? She said that she had dreamed about it and visualized it for weeks, even months. And then she said, "But I never saw myself finishing the race."

Visual/Auditory/Kinesthetic

Some athletes have a strong physical "feeling." They are more aware of how it "feels" than what it looks like. When they visualize, they don't really have a picture, they have a feeling, a gut reaction, a physical response or memory. This is what works for them and they find it hard to "see" anything, though they may still use the term "visualization." This also holds true for those athletes who experience their performance by how it sounds—the crowd, the voices within, the words of support from teammates, the music and rhythm they perform to or hear during a game, and so on. For them also there may be no real picture but rather a sound or rhythm in their mind that guides them in their performance.

The following questionnaire adapted from Instructor Magazine, January 1980,* will help you discover through which sense you tend to learn the best. There are ten incomplete sentences and three ways of completing each sentence.

1. My emotions can often be interpreted from my
   _____A. facial expressions
   _____B. voice quality
   _____C. general body tone

2. I keep up with current athletic events by
   _____A. reading the sports page thoroughly when I have time
   _____B. listening to the news or ESPN on TV
   _____C. quickly reading the sports page or spending a few minutes watching TV

3. If I wish to communicate with another person, I prefer
   _____A. face to face or writing letters

_____B. the telephone, since it saves time
_____C. to get together while working out or doing something physical

4. When I am angry, I usually
_____A. clam up and give others the silent treatment
_____B. am quick to let others know
_____C. clench my fists or grasp something tightly and storm off

5. When working out or competing, I
_____A. frequently look around to see the environment or my competition
_____B. tune into what's going on in my mind or think of a song
_____C. continually move around and physically get into it immediately

6. I consider myself
_____A. a precise and orderly person
_____B. to be a sensible person
_____C. to be a physical person

7. When at an athletic event, I
_____A. come prepared to keep times and scores
_____B. bring a small radio to hear the event better
_____C. move around a lot and don't stay in my seat

8. In my spare time, I would rather
   _____A. watch TV, go to a movie, or read
   _____B. listen to the radio or records or play an instrument
   _____C. participate in some physical activity

9. The best approach to disciplining an athlete is
   _____A. isolate the athlete by separating him or her from the group
   _____B. reason with the athlete and discuss the situation
   _____C. use acceptable forms of punishment such as benching or not competing in game

10. The most effective way to reward an athlete is
    _____A. written compliments or posting recognition for others to see
    _____B. oral praise to the athlete in front of others
    _____C. a pat on the back or a hug to show appreciation

Now count the number of checks in each A, B, and C column. If you have the most checks in the A column, you are primarily a visual learner. Having the most checks in the B column means you are mostly auditory or that you learn more through listening and sounds and rhythm. More checks in the C column indicate that you are a kinesthetic learner or a person who "feels" things and who likes a "hands-on" learning experience. If you have about the same number of checks in two or all three of the columns, you tend to use both or all three during any learning process.

For our purposes, the term visualizing can mean all three: visual, auditory, and kinesthetic. These are sensory ways by which we all learn and experience what we do and what happens to us. If you "visualize" yourself as a mediocre athlete, if you go into a workout or competition "seeing" yourself performing on an average level or slower or less perfectly than those around you, this is the way you will perform in reality. If, on the other hand, you "visualize" yourself performing well, feel yourself to be well prepared and ready, hear inner talk that supports you and your ability, you will produce the experience you are aiming for.

In an athletic event, visualizing yourself performing perfectly and achieving exactly what you want becomes that added edge you need to reach your peak performance. Each time you "see" yourself performing exactly the way you want with perfect form, you physically create neural patterns in your brain. These patterns are like small tracks permanently engraved on the brain cell. It is the brain that gives the signal to the muscle to move. It tells each muscle how to move, when to move, and with how much power. "Numerous studies have confirmed the fact that vividly experienced imagery, imagery that is both seen and felt, can substantially affect brain waves, blood flow, heart rate, skin temperature, gastric secretions, and immune response . . . in fact, the total physiology" (Houston, *The Possible Human*, 1982). It has been demonstrated that athletes who have never performed a certain feat before can, after several specific visualization experiences over a period of weeks or months, perform that event very skillfully. Ed Boyd, the women's gymnastics coach at the University of Oregon, told us of an experience he had. He taught a young gymnast a very difficult routine entirely by visualization. When she executed it perfectly the first time she tried, it frightened him so badly he didn't try visualization for years afterward!

Still it is vitally important that we do the physical training—that we move our bodies, strengthen our bodies, and train our bodies. Our performance will be tremendously more powerful if we have also trained our minds and created the neural patterns to help our muscles do exactly what we want them to do perfectly.

Content of a Visualization

A visualization starts at the beginning of your routine or workout. You must know what you want and what results you are aiming for in that particular visualization. It is good to have a knowledge of the "language" of your event, the terms and idioms of your sport. Along with this, you should have a clear picture of how it looks to perform your event perfectly. This you can get by watching the best athletes in your sport in person, on television, or looking at pictures in magazines or at posters. We suggest that you hang pictures of athletes performing your event to perfection where you can see them as often as possible. This will continually create the perfect picture in your mind, a feeling in your body, or important sounds or words and will keep you connected with what it will take for you to be the best you can be.

Once you have one of your goals and supporting affirmations firmly in mind, you are ready to begin creating the content of this specific visualization. In the beginning it helps to write it down as you go along so you incorporate as many senses as possible and so you can read it several times before you start. Also, many athletes find it helpful to have someone read it to them while they are in a relaxed state, or they record it themselves and listen to it later in a quiet and peaceful space.

See in your mind's eye the whole process and routine of your event in competition or in a significant workout in as much detail as possible. Visualize the competition area, the weather or the atmosphere of the room, the temperature, the sounds, the smells . . . everything. Imagine yourself warming up, stretching, talking to friends, concentrating—everything you do when you are about to compete or work out. Feel yourself to be totally relaxed, confident, and in complete control of your body and your mental state. If you notice that you are nervous, remember your affirmations—"I am strong and ready" and "I am relaxed and prepared"—and say them to yourself.

Imagine yourself beginning to compete, beginning your routine, the race, the match, the game. Notice everything you do, seeing it perfectly just the way you want it to be, just the way it should be done. If you make a mistake while visualizing your performance, go back, rewind, slow down the image in your mind, and do it over again, correctly, perfectly, exactly as you know it should be done. Experience yourself achieving your goal easily and with perfect control and know-how. Guide yourself through the whole event with perfection. See yourself successful. Be aware of how it feels and what it looks and sounds like to succeed, to achieve your goal. Allow yourself to experience achievement and success completely and fully by seeing, hearing, and feeling it all.

Now watch yourself as you warm down, relax and put on your sweats or as you head for the locker room. See yourself doing whatever you do after you compete or finish a major workout. Pay attention to the people around you, what they are saying and doing—anything that might be important to your visualization. Be sure to include all people or possibilities so you will be prepared for anything that may happen in the actual competition. If you are a runner and there might be other runners ahead of you, even though your goal is to win, "see" them in your visualization and see yourself catching and passing them. If you are a swimmer and there is a chance someone may false start, "see" yourself handling that situation perfectly, just the way you want to.

Think of simple key words or phrases you can recall during competition. These could be words such as "strong," "relaxed," "onfident," "smooth," "centered," and so on. If, while visualizing, you reach a point in your performance when you usually have trouble or self doubt, that is the time to use these key words or your affirmations. They will help you refocus and concentrate on your goal and let go of the negative energy and distractions into which you may slip.

When you are finished with your visualization, bring your attention back to your breathing and slowly begin to come back to your body and the space you are in. Remember your feelings of confidence, fitness, and mental toughness, those feelings of success and achievement. You can recall these images and feelings any time you choose. You may notice that your position has changed or that your breathing is different than when you started, or that you feel tired or as if you have all new energy. This "change" is due to the power of the visualization you have just experienced. Though you have competed only in your mind, visualizing can have such a powerful effect that your entire body feels as if you have actually, physically, competed. "Sports performance improves because the mind cannot distinguish between an imagined or real experience" (Syer & Connolly, Sporting Body/Sporting Mind, 1984). To your brain, a neural pattern is a neural pattern whether it is created by a physical act or a mental act. Your brain sends the message to the muscles and the muscles react.

In 1928, four young men were headed from New York to New Jersey on the subway to compete in a track meet between their college and one in New Jersey. They were the 400 Meter relay team. As they stood hanging onto the straps, one of the men suggested that each visualize his leg of the relay using his stop watch for timing purposes. Their goal would be to run each leg as close to ten seconds as possible. As they traveled, hanging onto the straps, they visualized each leg over and over, each runner performing to his peak. They reached the track and competed. They finished dead last. When they rested and began to discuss the race, they found that they were all so exhausted from having "run" their legs so many times between New York and New Jersey, they were too tired to run well in the actual competition!

For some athletes, visualizing on the day of competition is not beneficial. It may cause you to lose your focus. It may cause you to get too "hyped up" and therefore lose control. Or it may cause you to relax too much and not be keen enough for your peak performance. For most of us, visualizing works best during the week or weeks leading up to a specific competition. It is effective most when used at least once a day at a time when you are relaxed and undisturbed for at least 20 minutes. You may find that just before bed is a good time. On the other hand, it may be the worst time if visualizing excites and energizes you. One of the best times to visualize is while floating in a floatation tank. There are few times when you will be so relaxed and receptive to the "pictures" you produce in your mind. If you are an athlete who enjoys a regular massage, that is also a very good time to drop within yourself and go through your visualization. Be willing to experiment for a short time to find the most effective time and situation each day to quiet yourself, relax and visualize.

Creating Your Own Visualization

Here is how to write a guided visualization for your sport:

1. See, hear, and feel yourself performing your sport.
2. Write down or dictate into a recorder every detail you can see, hear, or feel.
3. Begin with arriving at the competition, going through your warm-up routine, and the few minutes before you start competition.
4. Go into vivid detail about the event and your experience of it, including the weather, the colors, the smells and sounds of the crowd, and the temperature and atmosphere.
5. In addition to detail, imagine yourself being totally relaxed, confident and in complete control of your body and your mental state. Feel the confidence, competence and control in your body and mind. Include your affirmations and simple key words that you can recall during competition.
6. Go through the whole event, seeing, feeling and hearing yourself at each significant point in the event. Feel yourself moving smoothly performing with strength and endurance, in total harmony with the environment and yourself.

7. After you finish visualizing your event, write statements of relaxation and remind yourself of your confidence, fitness level, and mental toughness. Tell yourself, "I am a winner."

8. Write everything out in a script, rereading it and editing it. Then dictate it at a slow speed into your recorder.

9. Listen to it for flaws, make changes in the script, and when it is satisfying to you dictate a progressive relaxation section (discussed in chap. 4) that you feel relaxes you best and follow with your finished script.

10. Listen to the finished tape as often as you wish (we suggest at least once a day) before a competition. Pick a quiet time and place where you will not be disturbed. In the evening or when you wake up are usually very good times.

Mental Trainer #9: Visualization

Break your visualizations into three basic parts: the beginning—before you compete; the middle—your competition; and the end—your victory lap, warm-down, return to locker room. The beginning should always be preceded by a progressive relaxation, centering, and letting go of your physical connections.

Goal:

Affirmations/Key Words:

Visualization:

Reread your visualization and be sure it includes the startof your competition, which means warming up, stretching, awareness of the competition area and the crowd and the environment in general. The visualization includes focusing on your goal and the outcome you wish to achieve. It includes everything important up to the moment you begin to physically compete—the gun sounds, the game begins, the clock starts.

The middle should consist of the competition itself: every move you make, all your strategy, everything up to and including the finish—the finish line, the final buzzer, or the end of your routine. It includes all the thoughts, feelings, physical moves, pains, sounds, and reactions.

The end encompasses all that happens after you have competed. This means the shouts of the crowd, your warm down, your victory lap, your reaction to yourself and those around you, any award you receive, joining your team, leaving the competition area. It consists of the reconnection with your body and the space you are in—the chair you are sitting in or the floor you lie on, the sounds around you, your present reality.

Be sure you have included as many senses as you can and have given yourself time to "see" each thing you feel is important to this visualization. Take your time to enjoy, to learn, to experience each movement and moment. See it all fully and perfectly and as completely as you know how . . . experience it exactly as you want it to be in reality.

Visualizations can also help your body deal with stress and injury. To see yourself relaxed and confident, dealing with any problem or situation effectively and with competence, will continually reduce your stress level and help you to take more control of your life in any competitive situation. When you are injured, visualizing your injury healing, seeing your body mending, feeling yourself to be in control and performing pain free and whole, will help your body create the image that becomes reality. Chapter 9 contains two useful visualizations for pain control and injury management.

The following is a guided visualization for goal achievement. More visualizations are included in chapters 7 and 11 as well as in Appendix B. They are good examples of the structure and wording for your visualizations.

A Guided Visualization for Goal Achievement

(Use the progressive relaxation outlined in chap. 4 once you have found a quiet and comfortable space.)

Let go of your body and time completely and begin to think of a time in your life when you knew that you knew . . . a time when you were "right on" and performed perfectly. See yourself at that time . . . notice what you look like, what you are wearing, who is with you, what sounds are around you, where you are. . . . Feel the environment and the energy. Begin to see yourself doing whatever it was you did when you knew you were right on . . . when everything worked perfectly . . . when you were in complete control and at your peak. Watch yourself and feel that feeling . . . connect with all the feelings you experienced as you achieved at your highest level

. . . perfectly . . . competently . . . exactly the way you wanted to . . . what did it feel like . . . sound like . . . look like? Let it all come back to you . . . let it in . . . know it again . . . the joy . . . the power . . . the pride and confidence . . . the completeness . . . the rush of knowing you were perfection . . . let it become part of you . . . part of your spirit . . . part of your being. Feel fully connected with it all.

Now, while completely involved with this absolute knowing, give yourself a word or short phrase that brings all these feelings, pictures, and sounds sharply into focus . . . a word or phrase that completely connects you with that time and those feelings when you knew that you knew . . . that you were perfect and right on . . . say the word or words to yourself several times . . . slowly . . . and allow yourself to experience your sense of power and wholeness . . . feel it in your whole body. . . .

Think of your goal . . . what you want to achieve now . . . the importance it has for you . . . remember how it felt to write it down and see it on paper. Begin to see yourself preparing to achieve this goal. Where are you and what do you look like? Are there other people there to assist you? What are they saying? Begin to go for your goal . . . see and feel yourself starting . . . moving toward your personal fulfillment. Give yourself permission to have it just the way you want it to be . . . see it perfectly as you move closer and closer to your goal . . . feel that excitement and rush that comes with doing something well, flawlessly, and with control . . . connect with your excellence as you reach and attain this important goal

. . . let yourself have it, feel it, see it, know it completely . . . say your special word or phrase . . . know those feelings . . . that power . . . see your peak performance . . . exactly the way you want it to be. . . .

Know that anytime you need it you can call up these feelings of perfection, competence, and power simply by saying your word or phrase . . . simply by reconnecting with your inner knowing and by seeing yourself at the moment of your peak performance. . . .

Experience yourself doing whatever you want to do now that you have reached your goal . . . be aware of how it feels to achieve . . . listen to the congratulations and hear the response of the world around you . . . allow yourself to experience the full impact of the outcome . . . the result of achieving your goal . . . let it in . . . relish it . . . touch it . . . let it be . . . have it all. . . .

Begin to let go of the image now . . . see it floating away from you . . . let it go . . . come inside to the peace of knowing and the quiet of your breathing . . . know that you have achieved at your highest level . . . you have succeeded . . . you have done it perfectly, just the way you wanted to . . . and breathe in deeply . . . bringing in new energy and peace . . . and . . . exhale slowly . . . releasing tiredness and tenseness. . . . breathe . . . slowly . . . breathe. . . .

Slowly reconnect with the chair you are sitting in or the floor you are lying on . . . move your toes . . . come back to your body . . . move your hands and fingers . . . and . . . quietly and gently open your eyes. . . .

"Gather the spirit of the hawk into yourself. Pull it

into the core of your being with your breathing. When you have the image push off and discover the hawk within" (McCluggage, The Centered Skier, 1983). It has been often said that what man is capable of seeing, he is capable of doing. We believe this to be true. Allow yourself to "see" everything you want, just the way you want it. With patience, work, training, and trust, you will have it in reality.

CHAPTER SIX

Mental Training for Peak Performance in Life

Our future success emanates totally and absolutely from our present mental attitude and self-concept. If you have accepted, as discussed in the introduction, that the pictures in our minds—how we "see" ourselves, our self-concept—have real and actual power, you can understand the importance of those pictures. If you "see" yourself as unacceptable in your peer group or your workplace, you will eventually manifest this in reality.

Sometimes it is difficult to know whether our mental training program for athletes preceded the idea of human peak performance or if it is a product of the personal growth movement. In either case the process is basically the same. The principles outlined in the first five chapters apply effectively to our lives in every way if we

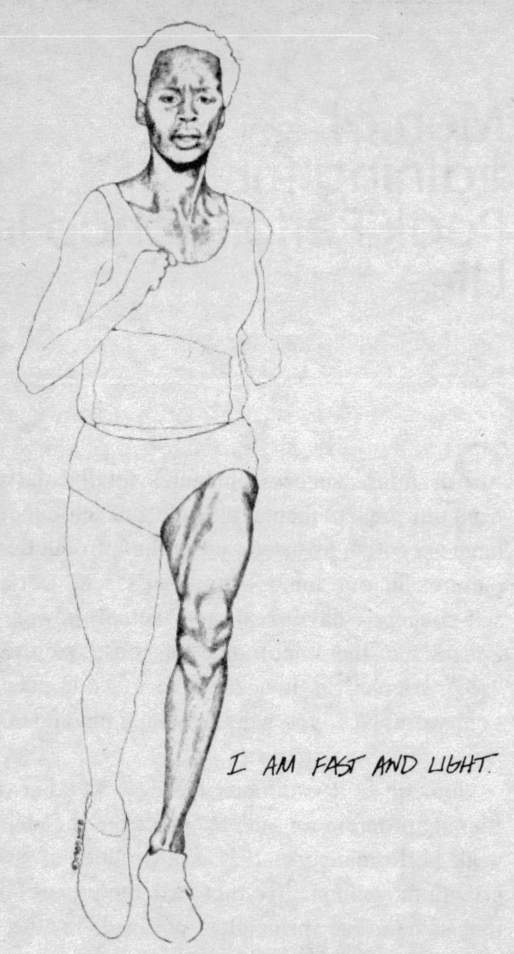
I AM FAST AND LIGHT.

are as dedicated to peak performance in our relationships, work, play, and so on as we are in our athletic endeavors.

What Do I Want?

We can have exactly what we want in our lives just as we can get what we want as an athlete. In life, as in athletics, the drive to achieve, to be all we can be, must come from within. It must be our choice. But first we must know what we want in life. This is a very difficult task, especially since our wants, needs, and desires seem to change like the seasons. Also, the changes we want to make often seem so huge and overwhelming that we get frustrated before we take even the first step. Therefore, it is most important to be, think, and feel in the moment, right now. What do you want in life right now, today, this week?

At this point, such a program may seem actually more difficult than if used only for athletics. And this is true. Many times our athletic wants and desires are much clearer. The vision of our athletic goals appears more tangible. "I want to run my first marathon." "I want to swim in open-water competition." These desires are straightforward and clear. But when it comes to desires in life, other emotions, other belief systems and other people's opinions, requests, and expectations come into play. We become afraid to be honest, afraid to commit, afraid to go against what we think we should want.

These are common stumbling blocks; they are not right or wrong. They can be handled and they can be overcome. We really can have what we want in life because we have sole responsibility for what we get in life. As we have said, the choice is always ours alone.

The first step is to want something. It can be more of what you already have, or it can be something entirely different. It can seem impossible or quite easy. It is important to be honest, to be true to yourself. Allow yourself to want anything you want. When you find yourself willing to really think of what you want, write these wants down just as they come. Put aside your fear of judgment, fear of failure, fear of rejection. Just think of everything you have ever wanted to be, to do, or to have. Write it down. As you write, imagine yourself being, doing, and having exactly what you want. Feel how it feels to set yourself free in this way. Notice if there is any inner talk. Is it positive or negative or perhaps both? Set your mind free and allow yourself everything.

Mental Trainer #10: What I Want

What I have always wanted in life:

That feels very good, doesn't it? Does it feel a little frightening too? What if you actually got everything you wanted? Take a moment again to "see" yourself being what you have always wanted to be; doing what you have always wanted to do, and having what you have always wanted to have.

Now begin to rank your desires in the order of the greatest importance to you. Assume for this moment that you can have it all. Decide which ones are the most important and number them. You are in no hurry. Think this over as clearly as possible realizing that wants sometimes change from day to day. Give yourself permission to be flexible. Your list might look like this:

3. to be thin

2. to be well educated

6. to make furniture

7. to get a big raise

1. to be prosperous

5. to own my own business

4. to have children

WHAT KEEPS ME FROM HAVING IT?

Now that you have a tangible idea of what you want in life, write down, starting with your most important wish, all the reasons why you "can't" have what you desire. We will return to our list to illustrate:

1. to be prosperous
   but . . . I don't have enough education.
   I don't know how to start.
   My mate would feel threatened.
   I would lose my present friends.
   I might fail.

Do this for the four desires you want the most. This will help you clarify what you consider your limits and will help you to understand what keeps you from having what you really want in life.

Mental Trainer #11: Roadblocks
Why I can't have what I want in life: *1* *But:*
2. *But:*
3. *But:*
4. *But:*

From these last two worksheets, you now have the material to begin the program defined in the first five chapters—that is, goal setting, affirmations, relaxation, visualization, and mental log keeping.

Take your three most important wants and form three goals. As discussed in chapter 2, focus specifically on what you want and the results you want to achieve. Be sure they are clear to you, that you know exactly what these goals mean to you and the results you really want. For example: "I want to be prosperous. This means to feel secure; to have enough money to feel free; to have a job I love doing; to be healthy and well accepted in my group of friends and workplace."

You may need to form "steps" or mini-goals as in chapter 2 to feel able to reach these goals and avoid feeling overwhelmed and frustrated or afraid to start.

For every "but" or reason why you cannot do, be, or have something, there is an affirmation that will help you turn this reason around, to see the fallacy of it, to let it go. Remember that a positive self-statement is present, positive, and personal and may not be exactly true at that moment. Therefore, "I don't have enough education" becomes, "I am intelligent and capable;" "My mate would feel threatened" becomes, "My mate listens and supports me, knowing that I care about him/her and his/her concerns." With every affirmation and positive visualization you use, you change old belief systems and form new ones that allow you to move and change, to achieve, to become, to do and to have what you want. And of course, the more you get out of your life, the more you have to give to yourself, to those you care about, and to the world in general.

Take with you your most important goal and find a quiet spot. Slowly bring yourself through the progressive relaxation exercise in chapter 4 and begin to visualize yourself attaining this important goal. Remember to use all of your senses. See yourself succeeding, hear the support and enthusiasm from yourself and others, feel the fullness of your heart and how it feels to accomplish this important desire. See it all from the beginning to the end. Notice how simple it can be. Step by step, you move toward your goal until you triumph. Allow yourself to experience it all. You can create your own visualization exactly as you want it to be. You are always in control, and it is positive and good.

Do this for each goal, one at a time, saying your affirmations as you watch yourself succeed. If you have a small tape recorder, you can record your visualization and then listen to it anytime you have a few minutes of quiet. Before you go to bed at night or when you are alone in your car are usually good times. Anywhere it is peaceful and you are relaxed is a good place to do your visualization.

As your wants and desires change, as you achieve your personal life-goals, new ones will take their place. Keeping a mental training log for life will help you remember and focus on these new goals as they occur to you. Each week or month there will be times you say to yourself or a friend, "That's something I have always wanted to do," or "Gee, I wish I could be like that person." Write these dreams in your log and when the time and desire presents itself, form your personal goals around them, one by one, and begin the process all over again.

If you are willing to risk and be dedicated to your mental training in your athletic endeavors, you will achieve your goals and eventually your peak performance. This is also true in life. The process is the same. Each new outcome, setback, and move forward is a learning experience and growth step. With each experience, each step, we go beyond our self-imposed limitations. We let go of our fear just a little and become willing to risk the next step.

CHAPTER SEVEN

Dealing with Problems and Blocks in Competition

As an athlete, what goes on in your mind before a competition? Are you afraid, excited, reluctant, anxious? How you handle these thoughts and feelings is important to your peak performance.

There is a law in psychology, the Yerkes-Dodson Law, that states in essence that if a little bit is good, a whole lot is not necessarily better. In other words, some anxiety, excitement, arousal, or anticipation is good for motivation, but too much decreases optimum performance. As an athlete, you must learn how to govern your emotions so they work for you and not against you.

The following are some of the more common problems or blocks in competition:

- negative self-talk
- choking/panic/freezing

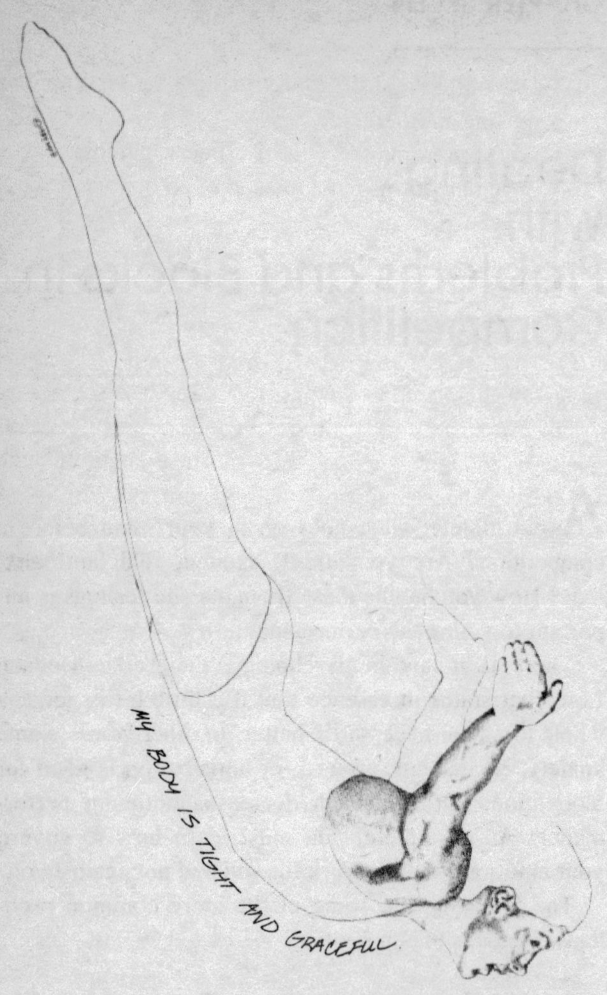
MY BODY IS TIGHT AND GRACEFUL.

- physical illness such as vomiting
- physical fatigue
- fear of failure, losing face, looking bad or stupid
- hurting another athlete
- pressure from others: coach, peers, parents
- psyching out yourself instead of an opponent
- nervousness

Negative Self-Talk

Most of the blocks we experience as athletes come from our negative self-talk and our belief systems about ourselves. Thoughts such as, "I don't have enough talent," "I'm not good enough," and "I am not disciplined enough," all stand in the way of our improvement. "I'm too young," "I'm too old," "I'm too tall," "I'm too short..."—all are limiting beliefs that keep us from achieving and help create the mind-set that makes us fearful in competitive situations.

Affirmations, when done consistently, help "reframe" or reprogram negative thought patterns. When you become conscious of what you are telling yourself in competition, you will begin to get a handle on how to get beyond the limitations of your mind. Everytime you notice yourself saying negative things, acknowledge that you are doing it, be patient with yourself, and say something such as, "Oh, there you go again; OK, let's get back to the positive," and begin saying some of your affirmations to yourself. "I am as good as anyone here."

"I enjoy competing." "I am strong and confident." "I am relaxed, alert, and ready to do my best." With practice, such statements will become reassuring and calming influences for your mental state during competition.

Choking/Panic/Freezing

When an athlete chokes, it is usually because she or he is fearful or angry. A tennis player, for example, may begin choking and missing every shot, and becoming more and more upset with himself or herself. The player has lost the "present" focus—that of staying in the present moment—and continues to think of the blown shots and mistakes made in the past. Combined with negative thinking, this process interferes with concentration, focus and confidence. To counter this block, the athlete must calm himself or herself, center inside, and shift concentration and focus to the present moment, focusing all mental attention on the upcoming shot. "Letting go" of the past and forgiving oneself for making errors is crucial in getting beyond the mistakes and no longer expending mental energy on the missed shots. This may take considerable willpower on the part of the athlete. But the habit of doing this consciously begins to overcome the old habits of negative thinking and self-blame, enabling the athlete to remain focused on the present moment of competition.

If the choking comes from fear, the athlete can use the same method. If you are scared, acknowledge the fear.

"Oh yes, here you are again and I know you feel scared," and so on. Once you have acknowledged this fear, proceed to imagine the fear as a ball, shrinking until it is a small manageable size. Instead of fighting or resisting the fear, acknowledge it and let it go. In this way you decrease your own resistance to it, and it will not get in your way. You control it instead of it controlling you.

After acknowledging the fear, take positive actions to begin thinking differently. Wallowing in the fear accomplishes nothing. By returning to a positive focus, you may want to begin thinking about the next move or shot you will be making. The affirmations of "I am alert and ready," and "I am centered, calm, relaxed, and ready" may help return you to a more controlled and peaceful state of mind.

When the fear is a pre-competition fear, it can be dealt with in a variety of ways. In addition to the positive and present focus and centering/relaxation techniques, you may want to remember a successful and pleasant experience, either in practice or competition, where you were in complete control and performing confidently and well. It may help to imagine a very successful practice you had so that you see, hear and feel all the bodily sensations you had when performing competently and successfully (see visualization in this chapter). All these feelings and sensations of competency and control will bring to your body a different physical state and will replace the fear with confidence and calmness. The reconnection with positive energy will reframe your current experience. You are remembering and recalling the confidence and well-being you felt in practice. This transfer of skills from practice to competition is an important tool for you to remember. You can, at any time, recall and summon the strength, power, and accuracy you felt during a good practice or previous competition.

"Breathe!" "What? Of course I breathe." Notice that when you are tense, uptight, fearful, or nervous, you begin to hold your breath. This is a natural response when one is not relaxed. As the tensions of the day increase, one tends to breathe more shallowly. One of the cornerstones of a state of relaxation is good, deep breathing. We often tease the athletes we work with by spontaneously asking, "Are you breathing?" And it is true—many times they are not breathing regularly. It will help you to begin noticing in any tense situation, either athletic or in your personal or work life, whether or not you are holding your breath or breathing shallowly. If you are, make an effort to breathe deeply and fully to create a more relaxed state of mind and physical well-being.

For pre-competition fears as runners, we personally have found it helpful to do progressive relaxation and a mental rehearsal/visualization of the course for at least a week before a big race. We then have control over the fear and can replace it with feelings of strength, relaxation, and familiarity. We say our affirmations to ourselves and see ourselves on the course, running strong and well within ourselves. We do this in our mind's eye, as we have discussed in previous chapters. Other runners we have worked with prefer to use our pre-recorded, guided visualization running tapes of specific races because they can focus their entire attention on the voices or words. Not having to exercise the mental discipline to do it within themselves, they relax, and let the tape do the work for them. Their minds wander less with this method, and the tapes help create a sense of peace, well-being, and anticipation.

People use our 10K or marathon race visualizations for other reasons too. We were surprised to learn that one man, a writer, listened to the marathon tape and was so energized by it that he sat down and wrote for three hours as fast as he could, turning out one of his best pieces of work. He said he felt exhilarated and full of energy. A woman runner listened to the tape as she awoke one morning, got up, and had the most beautiful run she had had in months, noticing all the trees, grass, dew, and flowers. We are often so unaware of our environment as we pass it by. Listening to tapes that describe sights, sounds, and internal feelings stimulates our awareness of our surroundings and makes us take notice. You may want to write your own script for a visualization, as suggested in chapter 5, and record it for yourself.

In case of panic or freezing, the athlete would do well to concentrate on breathing deeply and doing a short centering and focusing sequence while sitting, standing, or lying down. Close your eyes for a moment, bring your attention inward, and again call for the feelings of confidence and control from previous practices or events. Physical movement may help get rid of excess energy as well. Physical movement changes mental states, so activities such as stretching, jogging briefly or in place, or simply walking while being aware of your breathing should help you control feelings of panic. Noting your breathing is most important. Direct your attention at maintaining relaxed, full breaths.

Physical Illness Such as Vomiting

Some athletes are so fearful and upset that they throw up before a major competition. This long standing condition may be difficult to control. In addition to listening to relaxation tapes for a week or two before competition, and visualizing oneself as confident and in control of one's mental process and physical state, we recommend that the athlete work with a sports psychologist to learn how to balance the nervousness and fear with physical and mental relaxation, calmness, and a sense of well-being. Spending time alone before the competition may be a help or a hindrance, depending on the athlete. Some athletes need the quiet time alone to prepare themselves mentally using a series of relaxation procedures. Gymnasts often can be seen sitting alone and calming themselves or actively practicing their tricks alone in corners of the room before they compete. For others, being with someone else or a group has a calming or diverting effect that helps them stay more in control of their nervousness or pre-competition jitters. Athletes cope with the stress of competition in different ways. If a technique works for you, use it. If it is not working for you, be willing to try something new. Many times an athlete uses distraction just previous to competition. If this works, it's fine. Something else might work better. Be willing to try new ideas to discover what might help long-standing "mental blocks" in competition. Too often we continue to do what we have always done and invariably continue to get what we have always gotten. The key is to experiment until you find something that works even better for you. Be willing to risk and experiment with new techniques.

Physical Fatigue

Physical fatigue can be overcome mentally. Alberto Salazar, for example, has run himself almost to death's door, suffering from internal dehydration. He is so mentally tenacious that he runs until he drops. He tells himself that he may hurt but that the other guy is hurting too. So he runs harder. He wants to win and he is willing to go through pain to do so. Elite athletes acknowledge their pain and use it. Focusing on their form, breathing, or other body parts enables them to "handle" the discomfort and fatigue rather than being disabled by it. It is all part of what is called "mental toughness."

Concentrating on your breathing patterns will help you deal with physical fatigue. It will divert your attention from your muscles. Full in and out breaths oxygenate the system and revive tired muscles. Visualizing white light or gold energy coming into the lungs often brings a feeling of lightness to the body and a surge of new energy, refreshing the athlete. Imagining moving your body or legs and arms as if strings are attached and someone else is giving them the energy often helps. It is best to concentrate on body or form to keep your concentration focused on yourself in general and not on the specific area that feels tired or painful. Disassociation, while giving some relief, allows you only to survive. It does not facilitate maximum performance. Total concentration and focus on the present event is what is needed during peak performance. You continue to focus on the event, moment by moment by moment.

Fear of Failure, Losing Face, Looking Bad

A fear of failure, losing face, or looking bad creates an outward rather than inward focus. If we as athletes are concerned with these fears, we are focusing outside ourselves. Refocusing on our technique, our body, and our event, rather than on the crowd watching us, brings us back to the present moment and makes us internally focused. The successful athlete learns to ignore the crowd or uses its sounds as motivation to do better. "They are for me," "They want me to do well." Even reframing a negative crowd is possible. "I'll show them!" becomes a constructive tool. The old attitude of entering a competition under challenge, as defined in chapter 1, is quite acceptable in this case. The quiet inner knowing and confidence of the athlete sustains him or her even when the crowd may be booing. It is this inner reserve and confidence that brings forth peak performances. This state can be accomplished by the centering and breathing technique, saying affirmations, and feeling the relaxed and alert state of readiness for competition. Successful athletes know not to take the crowd's emotional displays personally but to remain within themselves and their performance.

Hurting Another Athlete

The fear of hurting another athlete is a common problem in contact sports. If, during your performance, you can remember that you are not responsible for another's experience, it will help you overcome this block. We have talked about blame and letting go of blaming others for your experiences. You have a responsibility to play fairly and ethically. Most athletes in contact sports are playing with the understanding that they may be hurt or may inadvertently hurt another. You are all playing with the same risks and acceptance of these risks. If you are clearly outmatched or are superior, it may be difficult. However, you play your best and want to win. It is important that you let the other athletes assume responsibility for their experience and performance. Fear of hurting another will hold you back and will be an impediment to your performance.

Pressure from Others: Coach, Peers, Parents

Often a block develops because of a poor relationship between a coach and an athlete or team. The coach must learn to handle athletes with different temperaments in different ways. A hardline, aggressive approach may work well with one athlete and not with another. Some athletes need support and positive feedback rather than criticism and negative feedback. Often this approach fails and some coaches are not willing to be "softer" with certain players. The athlete has control over how he or she handles what the coach is giving out.

We worked with a high school player who was constantly disturbed and upset because the coach was "riding" him. After a number of relaxation sessions, along with guided visualizations of himself playing well, hearing the coach's jibes and seeing the comments roll off him, he started to play better. Learning that he, the athlete, had control over how he took the coach's comments gave him some freedom, and he learned to ignore the negativity of the coach. Many coaches, while seeing themselves as realistic, subtly undermine their team's or athlete's confidence by their negative comments to the press. Simple statements such as "I was surprised we won" or "I'm not sure we're ready; we'll just go out and see what we'll do" are meant to be conservative and realistic. They are often seen and felt as negative by the athletes, who may feel fit and ready to go. After such comments, the athletes begin to feel a lack of support and often question themselves and their confidence.

Athletes sometimes tend to fool themselves into thinking they are better than they are and can't accept not playing or competing. They become antagonistic toward the coach, blame him or her, and generally are disgruntled and unhappy. Once athletes accept the responsibility for playing or not playing, they tend to improve and be more satisfied with their position. Again, we stress, you are in control of your feelings about the coach, the game, and the other athletes. Feelings of antagonism and anger directed at the coach or another athlete may sometimes help to motivate you; but usually these feelings interfere with peak performance and are counterproductive.

Other problems in competition often stem from peer pressure or pressure from parents. Not playing, not succeeding, and "riding the bench" all tend to undermine confidence and create fear about performing at all. If you can concentrate on watching other players and turning the experience of bench-sitting into learning, it will be to your benefit and will keep you from psyching yourself out and putting yourself down. If you see yourself as a "loser," you will create this atmosphere around you. If you are "unattached" to playing or not playing, you will feel better about yourself and won't be riding a roller coaster of emotions. Make a game out of watching the best athletes or players in great detail—their form, how they breathe, their temperament, all the nuances you can see, hear, or feel about their performance. Let those who are pressuring you know that you are learning from the best and that it is important to you—it is part of your training. Imitate what you like about their style and learn something new. In this case, it benefits you to be "outwardly" focused. You can learn a lot from others while you are waiting your turn to play or compete.

Supporting your team or fellow athletes with enthusiasm helps you stay "up." Many times, being supportive is as important as participating. Let go of your ego, focus on the moment, and support others as well as yourself regardless of what your peers or parents expect of you.

Psyching Out Yourself Instead of an Opponent

In psyching up yourself, you psych out your opponent. Marilyn King, an American pentathlete on the Olympic team in 1980, talked about how she entered the last event, the 800 meters, jumping around, full of energy, ready to go. Part of it was to psych herself up and to get her energy moving and the other part was to intimidate her opponents who were also dog-tired. One athlete said to her later, "I hated seeing you with so much energy when I was so tired. It was depressing. You always looked confident and ready."

Mary Decker has talked of seeing a "look" in her opponents' eyes. "They were almost always running for second place." It is important to create upbeat images of yourself and for yourself. Look, feel, and act confident.

Look ready and calm and in complete control. "I am strong, powerful, and quick." "I am relaxed and confident." "I am full of energy and life." "I am as good or better than anyone at the starting line." All these affirmations create positive intent and consciousness. Power words such as light, easy, fast, accurate, calm, relaxed, centered, strong, and powerful help create a positive image and feeling within you. Affirmations can be important in shifting your focus from the negative frame of mind you may fall into when you push to your physical limits. Something as simple as "This is good for me" said during a hard workout when you feel fatigue can keep you going.

Summary

For success in overcoming blocks in competition you must practice the following:

- relaxation, centering, and focusing before and during competition
- transforming feelings of competence and ability from practice or past competitions to feelings of confidence in present competition
- visualizing yourself competing with control and confidence.
- turning anger and disappointment into productiveness and positive feelings, not depression

- taking total responsibility for your behavior and not blaming others for your mistakes or losses
- letting others be responsible for their own experience
- using affirmations for self-support and confidence

Visualization for Dealing with Competition Blocks

The following visualization may help you learn to bring the feelings and experience of confidence and competence to any competitive situation. First practice the progressive relaxation described in chapter 4. Then you may begin with the following guided visualization.

Feel yourself to be centered, at peace, and relaxed. With your mind's eye, begin to see yourself at a workout where you were performing at your absolute best... where you were performing perfectly and you felt competent and confident... a time when you absolutely knew that you knew and you were in complete control of your body and mind... a time when you knew completely that you were right on... a workout where you were at your peak physically and mentally... you were in control and having fun... there was no pressure and it was easy. See yourself at that workout right now. Notice what you are wearing and how the people around you look. Become aware of how it felt deep inside of you when you knew you were absolutely right on...

competent . . . in control . . . perfect. Take a look at those feelings . . . you felt comfortable and relaxed . . . after all, it was just a workout . . . you were loose. What were you saying to yourself?

As you become aware of those feelings, choose a word or a short phrase that reminds you of those feelings . . . a word that makes you think of those feelings . . . makes you feel those feelings again. Picture the word in your mind . . . say it over to yourself . . . remember the feelings. And then think of your perfect performance . . . the way you looked . . . what you heard . . . how you felt. Feel the experience deeply and say the word over to yourself. Notice how the word brings back that experience of fun and ease and makes you feel and see yourself at your peak . . . performing perfectly. Say the word over to yourself and allow yourself to feel those feelings of being absolutely perfect.

Now . . . think of your goal in your next big competition and begin to see yourself there . . . at your next competition. The goal you have in mind is very important. Say this goal over in your mind. When you have the goal well in mind, begin to see yourself achieving this goal and remember the relaxed, easy feelings you had at that great workout. Start at the beginning of the competition . . . watch . . . listen . . . feel and smell everything you can as you move closer and closer to achieving this goal. It is as easy as a workout . . . no pressure, no tightness . . . you are smooth and in control . . . relaxed and having fun. Remember your affirmations now . . . say them over to yourself . . . say those phrases that support your goal . . .

say your word . . . watch yourself coming closer and closer to your goal, feeling comfortable, having fun . . . you are light and smooth and loose. Notice how it feels inside . . . what you are saying to yourself . . . feel it in your heart . . . remember the special word you just gave yourself and how it connects you to all those feelings of competence . . . confidence and well-being, relaxation, ease and strength . . . allow yourself to stay in those feelings as you see yourself finally reaching your goal . . . competing at your highest level . . . feeling good . . . having fun. Become aware of what happens now that you have succeeded. What is happening around you? What is happening within you? Are people congratulating you . . . are you alone? Feel the peaceful inner knowing that you have done what you set out to do . . . you have done it well . . . it feels just as easy to compete as it feels at a good workout. Allow yourself to experience all of those feelings and the knowledge and success. . . .

Know that anytime you want to call up those feelings again . . . anytime you want to have that sense of competency, ease, relaxation and enjoyment, all you have to do is center yourself, take a deep breath, and say your special word or phrase to yourself to reconnect with those feelings. . . . Now begin to watch the scene of your successful competition float away from you . . . watch it becoming dimmer . . . let it go . . . you remember how it feels . . . know that you are perfectly capable of achieving it anytime you choose as you begin to come back into the peace in your mind . . . the relaxation in your body . . . the quiet of the room . . . come back to your breathing . . . notice how steady it is . . . breathe deeply into your belly . . . filling your chest with air . . . hold it . . . and let it go. When I count to three you may come back into the room . . . one . . . you begin to move a little and reconnect with your body . . . two . . . move your arms and legs . . . three . . . you may open your eyes when you are ready. . . .

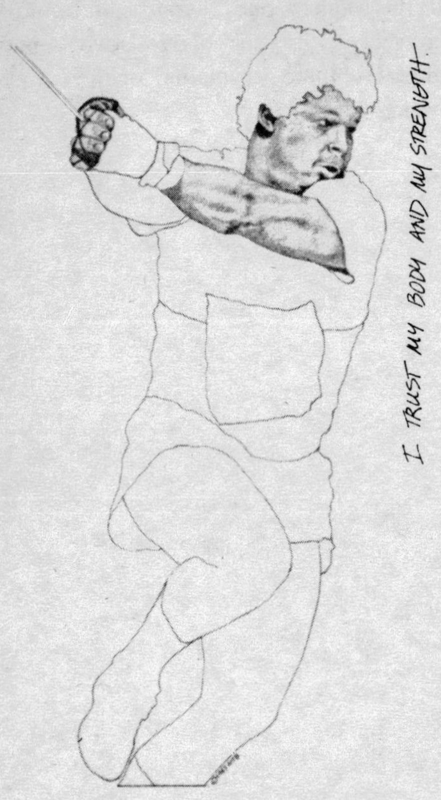
I TRUST MY BODY AND MY STRENGTH.

CHAPTER EIGHT

Psychological Issues of the Female Athlete

Anything we can do as women in education to encourage girls and women in sports is an important step in helping females to view themselves, not only as athletes, but also as women whose self perception includes physical strength, competence, grace and confidence without apology, without qualification, and without compromise.

Patricia S. Griffin

"It's not feminine to sweat . . . to be a good athlete . . . to be aggressive . . . to beat the boys/men. . . ." When it comes to being athletes, women have been conditioned by society to believe they are mentally and physically inferior to men. Because the attributes that lead to athletic success—determination, aggressiveness, leadership, competitiveness, self-confidence—are generally considered masculine, the need to adhere to an acceptably feminine role has discouraged girls and women from participating in sports. Women are taught that they are not strong enough or fast enough or mentally tough enough to be great athletes. Even in the 1984 Olympics, women were not allowed to run either the 5000 meters or the 10,000 meters, and only in 1984 was the first women's Olympic marathon held amid much controversy and resistance. Society has felt it must "protect" women from themselves and physical injury in sports. No wonder women doubt themselves.

Not surprisingly, the female athlete has special needs in the area of sports psychology and mental training to overcome this negative programming and self-talk she has internalized since childhood.

The Issues

Several significant issues face women of all ages. These seem to be the main ones:

- to learn that aggressiveness, self-confidence, competitive achievement, and femininity can go hand in hand
- to feel OK about beating one's friends, both male and female
- to learn that it is acceptable to take time from family and the home for oneself and one's athletic training and competitions

- to stop worrying about what others think of one's commitment and performance
- to deal with society's stereotyping and attitudes toward sexual orientation

At what age do women learn to stop competing and start limiting themselves to save someone else's ego or to fit into their peer group? Boys are expected to participate in sports and are actually pushed by their fathers and peers to be athletic. This will bring them validation and reward. Young girls are urged to be "little ladies" and are usually recognized and rewarded for feminine, house- and family-related pursuits. In college many girls lower their self-expectations and ambitions to avoid the disapproval of their male peers who may feel threatened by too much competence and ambition in a woman. "Independence, aggressiveness and competitive achievement, all of which may threaten the success of heterosexual relationships, are often given up by adolescent girls in order to increase their attractiveness to boys" (Bardwick & Douvan, *Ambivalence: The Socialization of Women*, 1972). The age when a female athlete begins to hold herself back and mold herself according to the desires of society and her peers depends on the individual. It is exciting to find in the younger generations a willingness in many girls to forge ahead, to fly in the face of outdated concepts to perform at their highest level. They are willing to take risks to reach their peak athletic performances, as we all must be wiling to do. As a female athlete, what are some of your issues and concerns?

Mental Trainer #12: Female, Athletic, and Proud	
My Female Athletic Issues:	
Does it Help Me or Hinder Me?	*How:*
Does It Help Me or Hinder Me?	*How:*
Does It Help Me or Hinder Me?	*How:*

Aggressiveness

Aggressiveness is learned most easily by pushing oneself to act "aggressively" even when it feels uncomfortable at first. We do not mean being obnoxious, loud, or cocky.

Aggressiveness means asserting oneself, being an initiator, being "pro-active" rather than reactive or simply responding to someone else's initiative or move. Rushing the net, rebounding for the ball, surging in a race, and intercepting a shot are all examples of assertive and aggressive behavior. You can be aggressive without being hostile or angry. You are merely initiating a play or move instead of waiting to respond.

Many coaches resort to making their players angry to arouse their energy and aggression. This works to a certain extent because the player goes into the "challenge" mode of "I'll show you!" The athlete becomes a champion not because of an "OK-ness" in her mind, but because of an attitude of "I'll prove myself to you, and I'm right, you're wrong." This may work. However, this technique often backfires when an athlete is under pressure. When the pressure gets too great, anger is not enough and the athlete loses mental control and focus. There is nothing left to rely on. Often as a result the team chokes or the athlete tightens and loses her rhythm.

Dealing with anger is a crucial issue for all athletes, both male and female. Females are often uncomfortable being angry or having someone angry with them or both. Women are taught that their anger is unacceptable and unlady-like. Also, many women are not used to conflict or confrontation. Women involved in sports that involve these components will often need special teaching. Women can learn that it is as acceptable for them as for men to feel and express their anger and frustration when in competition. The objective for both is to be the master of one's emotions, to acknowledge the feelings and then to drop them, refocusing on the task at hand and staying in the present moment. Letting go and dropping the anger you feel is crucial in becoming a great athlete. Mary Decker felt anger, frustration, and pain when she fell during her bid for the gold medal in the 3000 meter race at the 1984 Olympics. Society in general, and the press in particular, judged that her all-too-human reaction not acceptable behavior from America's "sweetheart." If one looks deeper into this attitude, what was being said is that it is not acceptable for her, a woman, to have these emotions. John McEnroe's behavior, not to mention that of several basketball coaches, while not ultimately acceptable, is publicly more acceptable than was Mary Decker's. Within twenty-four hours, Mary was willing to give a press conference with her emotions far more under control. She showed many signs of a willingness to put it behind her, to let go, certainly of the anger if not the frustration with herself, her choices and the situation as a whole. Jim Ryun fell in a heat of the 1500 meters in the 1972 Olympics in Munich but was not confronted by the press within minutes of his fall as Decker was. He put Decker's situation into some perspective when he said "As I saw her on television, I was thankful for one thing: I didn't have a press conference immediately afterward. It gave me a little time to gain some composure" (*Runner's World*, Feb. 1985). Extreme emotions are natural to all humans, especially in highly stressful situations. We do not advocate a display of emotion that destroys an athlete's focus and eventually his or her performance. We do support being aware of all emotions, acknowledging their existence, and using constructive control.

Competing with Friends

Competing with and beating one's friends and teammates seems to be a real concern for young college women. In interviewing an outstanding, national-class runner, we listened with fascination to her story about an important race with a teammate. "We were running together and I was in front, leading most of the way. She kept surging to pass me and every time she got even with me, I picked up the pace so she couldn't pass. This happened several times and on the last home-stretch, I kicked and won. I felt terrible about it and apologized to her afterward. She didn't seem to mind, but it made me very uncomfortable because she was my friend and I didn't want her to be angry with me."

We discussed this "fear" of hurting or angering her friend with her and reframed the race for her. We looked at it from a different perspective: "You are here to compete and you were being fair. This is the whole idea of competition. Your friend wanted to win too and that is what she was trying to do. Both of you were pulling and pushing each other to run, helping each other to achieve a peak performance, to run better and faster." She agreed and went on to the best performances of her college career, setting numerous PRs in her event all season and in Europe. She became a fine competitor, aggressive yet controlled and "fair," optimizing her substantial talent and ability. She has brought her mental ability up to par with her physical ability.

Taking Time for Oneself

Women have long been taught to be "care givers" to others. For women age 35 and older, taking time for oneself is often felt to be selfish and self-indulgent not only by the family but by the woman herself. The family should come first. However, research has shown that the more a person nurtures himself or herself, the more care and nurturing he or she can give to others. This self-care helps restore the internal energy system of the person. It "fills up the well" so more love and energy can be given to others.

Activities that furnish a woman with athletic success enhance her self-concept and confidence. Athletic training and competition help develop a sense of accomplishment and can be an excellent opportunity for the family to return some of the support and love they have received.

Many families put pressure on the female parent who becomes athletic to stay at home more to meet the family's needs. A subtle underlying guilt-trip from the family may undermine athletic desire and achievement. Dealing with this attitude can be difficult. The more a family "gives back" love and support, the more the female athlete will be able to perform at her best without distraction. Asking the family for support such as allowing guilt-free training time, attending competitions, and assuming some of the responsibilities at home can do wonders in creating family unity and pride. Honest communication from the woman to her family about how important it is to her that they support her athletic participation can help build an enduring and broad base of family harmony.

Worrying about the Audience and Others

While interviewing female athletes from team and individual sports we learned of another major performance issue. Many women had problems with their concentration and focus because they were so concerned with what the audience was thinking about them. Gymnasts and tennis players often had this problem. They were self-conscious and worried about how they looked when performing. They were concerned about their acceptability as compared to someone else. They were concerned about making a fool of themselves and losing face.

The moment any athlete shifts mental focus from self to others, concentration is lost. Most women are not self-focused. They have learned that it is more acceptable to be outwardly focused, to be concerned about the other person. Loss of concentration results in missed shots or falling off the beam or loss of rhythm and form. This problem is widespread among athletes who must perform solo, though it is not so prevalent in team sports where the group energy and group identity help an individual melt into the "team" image. By focusing on her form or routine, the female athlete can eliminate this problem and improve her concentration.

Fear of Being Thought Unfeminine or Gay

One infrequently discussed concern of female athletes has to do with being thought gay or homosexual because one is a "jock." Many coaches and athletes are very fearful of being thought gay and adopt homophobic responses. One coach was so concerned with his team's "feminine" image that he would not publicly allow his team to be associated with any sports professionals whom he had heard were gay or bisexual. This is a sad situation not only because it perpetuates the paranoia but because it robs a team of skilled professional services. Should an athlete happen to be gay, he or she might live in fear and terror of being "found out" while working with a coach who displays this fear.

While it becomes acceptable to be feminine and a fine athlete, it should also be acceptable to be a fine athlete and set one's own standards of femininity. The female athlete should nurture a strong sense of power, personal identity, and self-confidence. Part of a coach's job is to promote and support these psychological characteristics in his or her athletes. One's sexual orientation has very little connection with athletic performance and should be left to one's personal discretion.

Motivation

One issue we stumbled on while talking to coaches had to do with motivating the female athlete to work hard and take her performance or the team's performance seriously. For some reason that is not well understood, some coaches of team sports have a difficult time motivating their athletes, getting the athletes to practice as hard as they need to if they are to beat more "upbeat" teams. Coaches are frequently frustrated trying to figure out how to get their players to play hard and aggressively. Why athletes play is an important issue. They may be playing for the wrong reasons and therefore pulling down team morale.

Those athletes who succeed at the highest levels play for the sheer love of it. It is what they want to do. But many women play for other reasons, and it is important to be aware of these reasons if you wish to perform and compete at your highest ability. These reasons include:

- to impress my father/parents, brother, boyfriend
- to keep my scholarship and stay in school
- to keep my weight down
- fear of rejection by my coach, father/parents, peers
- being judged as a sissy

Take a look at your motivation. Why are you an athlete, and why do you work hard to do your best and to compete at your highest level?

Mental Trainer #13:
Motivators

My Sport:

Why I Compete (in order of importance):

1.
2.
3.
4.
5.
6.

How I Feel about My Sport and My Reasons:

As we work with teams and individuals who are confronting a motivation problem, anger and frustration between the athletes and the coach and between individual team members often surfaces. We encourage the athletes and coaches to share their concerns, needs, and fears in open-minded, honest communication sessions. We act as facilitators for this process. Their willingness to put themselves in a position of vulnerability with one another usually clears the air for all concerned, so that energies can be focused on performance and competition rather than personal issues. We have experienced much success using this method of conflict resolution. The teams' achievements and motivation have grown and expanded.

Summary

Regardless of the old-fashioned belief systems built around femininity, other peoples' judgments, beating a friend or teammate, allowing yourself permission to train and achieve or sexual orientation, the truth is that:

- It is OK to be a woman and a champion.
- Women are strong enough and fast enough to be outstanding athletes.
- A woman can be beautiful, feminine, and a great athlete.
- Your personal self-concept is all that matters.
- Being physically active and fit is healthy, acceptable, and desirable in today's generation.

Dr. Porter's Research on Women Runners

Before forming Porter Foster, Ms. Foster was a writer, athlete, and artist. Dr. Porter, also an athlete, did numerous studies of women runners. In Dr. Porter's studies, she found that 96 percent of the women over 35 had not been active in any kind of sport at all in high school. Women's athletics were almost non-existent at the time. Through running, these women began experiencing physical success. They felt free in both body and mind. Fortunately, today's young women have a variety of sports from which to choose, and their role models in sports are increasing each year. More women are making more money and achieving status in the sports world. They are feeling good about themselves and their abilities.

The following is a synopsis of Dr. Porter's research:

In 1979, while I was training for my first marathon, I began to look for articles about women and running. Aside from Joan Ullyot's book, *Women's Running*, and a couple of others, information focused mainly on world-class female runners rather than average and intermediate women runners. For three years, I collected large amounts of descriptive and psychological data on women competing in women's races in the Northwest. I analyzed data on depression, anxiety, relationship satisfaction, and safety (fear of attack). The data described here represents a synopsis of my original study of 218 female runners who participated in a Nike OTC 10K women's race in Eugene, Oregon. I wanted to know what other women were thinking and doing with regard to their running, so I asked them everything I ever wanted to know. I am indebted to these women who so kindly and carefully filled out my first questionnaire. Many not only completed the survey but wrote extra pages with details of their experiences.

The 218 respondents who returned the first questionnaire ranged in age from 12 to 59. To my surprise, 50 percent of them were over the age of 30. Of the total group, 38 women had also completed marathons, and 58 percent of these marathoners were over the age of 30.

The questionnaire contained demographic data on the age, weight, height, occupation, and highest schooling completed. Data was also collected on training patterns, psychological changes experienced, diet, psychological aspects of running, satisfactions gained from running, and using running as a way of coping with stress.

THE TOTAL GROUP

The average woman completing the survey had run longer distances (6 miles/day or more) for approximately 18 months. So the group as a whole was well conditioned aerobically. About 50 percent of the respondents kept journals of their running activities. The majority were not doing sprints, intervals, or fartlek in training. For the women over 30, at least 50 percent had lost ten pounds or more after they had begun running longer distances. Most runners ran every three or four days on the average, and mostly in the morning hours.

PSYCHOLOGICAL CHANGES AND SATISFACTIONS FROM RUNNING

Over 90 percent of the group felt that running had

- increased their positive self-image
- made them feel better about their own bodies

- made them feel more comfortable with their own aging process

Of the respondents, 65 percent felt that running had improved their attitude about aging in general, while 35 percent felt that their attitudes about aging had remained virtually the same. Eighty percent felt that their running helped them cope better with stress. The psychological satisfactions that the majority felt they had gained from running were

- physical activity
- achievement
- improved body image
- weight control

The majority of the respondents from 30 to 45 years of age reported that these satisfactions from running were also the most important to them. The age group from 45 to 49 listed weight control as the most important satisfaction, followed by physical activity, achievement, and relaxation. The group from 50 to 59 also listed physical activity, achievement, and relaxation as the most satisfying rewards of running.

In answer to a question about ways they might use running as a coping skill, 75 percent of the women used running as a release from tension, 58 percent used it as a relaxation tool or for relief of depression and mood improvement, and 50 percent used it just for relaxation purposes.

Most of the responses concurred with my personal experiences. These women had never looked or felt better, either physically or emotionally. They felt wonderful and very alive.

I also found it interesting that the 45 to 49 age group had listed weight control as the most important satisfaction. As the body metabolism slows down, it needs some help in burning fat. Weight loss in women runners over 40 ranged from 11 to 18 pounds on the average.

THE MARATHONER SUBGROUP

I decided to look at the marathoner subgroup in depth. Were there differences between female marathoners and non-marathoners? Yes, there were some differences, and there were also some similarities.

DIFFERENCES

Of the 218 respondents, 38 had completed at least one marathon. Of the marathoners, 58 percent were from the ages of 30 to 59. Many of their responses were the same as the general groups. The differences were the following

- The majority of the marathoners ran at least 40 miles a week.
- They had been running for a longer period of time than the other group—about three years on the average.
- The majority of the marathoners also did sprints

and/or intervals at least once a week. Most did sprints or fartlek two to three times per week.

- Of marathoners, 79 percent reported having lost an average of 12 pounds since running longer distances.
- The majority (62 percent) of the marathoners reported that they had liked running as beginners. Many reported they liked running as beginners because it was something they could do completely on their own with no help from anyone else.

SIMILARITIES

The total group of marathoners felt that running had increased their self-confidence and positive self-image. They felt good about their bodies. Fifty-nine percent also felt much more comfortable with their own aging process. They rated the most important psychological satisfactions gained from running as follows:

- physical activity
- physical achievement and challenge
- weight control
- improved body image
- time to think
- competition

The marathoners used running as a coping skill most frequently to

- release tension
- relieve frustration
- improve mood
- relax
- do problem solving and mull over the day's events

In additional studies I conducted on women over 35 who ran 10K races, I came out with a mood profile almost identical to that of the elite male marathoner profile from a well-known study conducted by William Morgan. Like elite male marathoners, my female subjects showed tension, depression, anger, and fatigue levels far below the population norm, while energy levels were much higher. No previous researcher had looked at that for women. I found it remarkable that women over 35 had that same profile. It means that you don't have to be a world-class, young, male runner to have the same psychological benefits.

Summary

The original study showed that women between the ages of 30 and 60 have been using running as a coping skill to deal with frustration, tension, and to increase relaxation. Although the majority did not report using running for relief of depression, they did report that when they were not able to run for periods of a week or two due to illness or other factors they became depressed and irritable.

The vast majority did not enjoy running as beginners, but after they had increased their mileage to five or six miles per run they began to enjoy the benefits. They recommended going on a run when one is feeling tense and frustrated.

All in all, the total group of women used running for physical activity, for improving body image, for weight control, and for relaxation purposes. As a result, they seemed more comfortable with their own aging process. Much of the psychological benefit for women over 35 was improved body image. They liked their bodies. How many women over 40 or 50 do you know who don't like their bodies? I had a terrible time with aging when I was younger. When I was 29, I thought it was the end of the world. When I turned 30, I thought I was supposed to become a matron! That has changed for thousands of women. Now we think, "Oh boy, a new age division!"

CHAPTER NINE

Coping with Injury and Pain Control Techniques

Perhaps you have learned this mental training easily. Your physical body is improving, your mental "body" is improving, and then, WHAM, you're injured. Then what?! Coping with injury is one of the most difficult parts of training. To see your teammates and competitors exercising, competing, practicing their techniques, and having fun while you sit on the sidelines; to feel yourself losing your stamina and strength; to begin believing you are losing your edge—all this can be depressing at best. What can you do to combat and cope with your feelings of helplessness and frustration? The mental training program described in this book can be applied to the healing process. You can develop the following:

- a mental training program for dealing with injury
- a visualization program for healing the injury

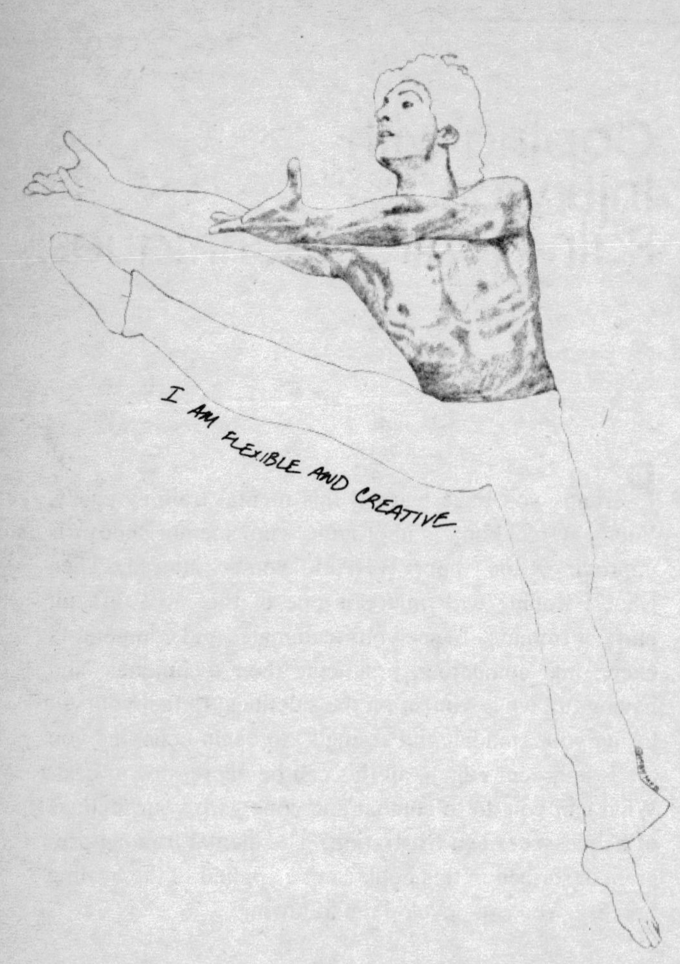
I AM FLEXIBLE AND CREATIVE.

- an inner-guide process to help you heal yourself
- pain-control techniques for injuries

In ancient healing and spiritual traditions, the power of positive mental imagery was often a major part of the healing process. An important element of self-healing is a mental image that projects a positive future outcome. The visualization you imagine stimulates your mind and your body and creates a positive intention for healing. When you picture yourself well and whole, you have begun the process of creating the positive "you" of the future. When injured, you can visualize a time in the future when you have regained your fitness and health. As with all visualizations, you should be careful to include as many visual, auditory, and kinesthetic cues as possible to create a complete and whole picture. Be specific and concrete.

Mental Training Program for Dealing with Injury

In creating your mental training program for injury, begin with the goal-setting exercise and create physical healing goals for yourself. For example:

Goal: "I wish to be performing pain free within the next three weeks. I want to be strong and able to work out with a healthy body in three weeks."

After writing your goals—two short term, two intermediate and two long-term—write at least five affirmations for each goal. For example:

1. I am performing pain free.
2. I am strong and healthy.
3. I am healing more and more every day.
4. I am healthy and whole.
5. I am now working out pain free.

Mental Trainer #14: Self-Healing
Short-Term Goals for Healing *Affirmations:*
Affirmations:

Intermediate Goals for Healing *Affirmations:*
  Affirmations:
Long-Term Goals for Healing *Affirmations:*
  Affirmations:

Pick the five affirmations that are most important to you, write them on 3 × 5 cards, and put them around the house where you will see them often. Also, read them and say them to yourself at least twice a day, preferably in the morning and before bed at night. These messages will begin to counteract your negative thoughts about your injury. They will begin to change your focus from one of frustration and centering on the pain and problem to one of self-control, healing, and wholeness.

After a week or so you will notice that your self-talk has become more and more positive. We often say negative things to ourselves that we would not permit others to say to us. Positive images and self-affirming statements have tremendous positive mental power.

The third step in our healing program is, of course, the visualization process.

Begin with the relaxation process as usual. Then continue to mentally visualize yourself practicing, improving your form and technique, performing well and with strength and endurance. See yourself well-bodied and whole. Imagine yourself performing exactly as you want to perform, without pain or weakness. Visualize your entire event and performance perfectly. Mentally practice your entire workout routine, imagine yourself in competition, see yourself well-bodied and winning. Watch videotapes of yourself performing or watch technique videos of your event, imagining yourself as the focal point. See your body performing and succeeding. Instill yourself with desire. Desire to recover, to be the best, to win. What you want or desire athletically must be so compelling and powerful that nothing will stand in your way. This desire is such a powerful energy source that it will enable you to achieve anything you want to do.

You may want to watch practice (though many athletes hate to watch when they are injured). Reframing your attitude while watching will help you learn to support teammates or fellow athletes. Pretend to yourself that you are the coach or a camera and watch each performer, analyzing his or her form, technique, strategies, and any weaknesses or strengths. This will help you later in your competition with them as well as help you focus on their present level of skills instead of your frustrations.

Again, keep a mental training log—this time for your injuries and how you cope with "temporary" retirement. One athlete said that she noticed she had gone through all the stages of loss (outlined by Elisabeth Kubler-Ross) while she was injured: denial, anger, bargaining, depression, acceptance. This is a healthy process as long as one does not stay stuck in a stage such as anger or depression. One can reach acceptance as well as achieve a positive future image of oneself performing again.

Leann Warren, the University of Oregon NCAA 800/1500-meter champion in 1982, is a great example of the power of positive thinking and visualization. After five surgeries in two years, she is not only running again but she is racing without pain. Her last surgery was January 4, 1984. She finished one second behind Kathy Hayes in the National Cross Country Championships in November 1984 and consistently raced faster with each passing month. Leann is a master of positive mental training. In an interview with Leann, we asked her how she coped mentally with the injuries and surgery and how she kept going in the face of all odds.

"It wrecked my Olympic hopes for 1984. I was upset. I cried. After Tom Heinonen (Oregon women's track coach) and I talked a while, I just started focusing on other goals . . . the World Championships, other meets, and world records. I look ahead now. Tom told me, 'You're 22. You have years ahead of you. Look at the long term. Get healthy now. Just get healthy.' He really helped me a lot. My parents were great too. They just wanted to see me happy again and for me to do whatever I needed to make me happy. A lot of people just faded away. Initially, that upset me. It was hard for people to talk to me because conversation focused around running, so it was awkward. It was hard after running so well and being so successful not to be able to do it. I wanted to do it so badly. I really struggled with anger. I hated hearing people complain about training. I wanted to run and couldn't and they were complaining. This was just a stage I went through. I realized that in the long run I'll be a stronger person after going through all this. I really proved to myself that I don't give up. I wasn't able to do the running part but I didn't lose anything physically. I lifted weights and biked and swam. My fitness remained at a real high level.

"In terms of mental training, I have always used the mental techniques the team was taught. I imagine the injury getting better, I counsel myself, I get myself to stop worrying. We did formal relaxation sessions in high school; I use it unconsciously now. Larry Standifer and Dr. Stan James at the Eugene Orthopedic and Fracture Clinic have helped me a lot in terms of support and treatment. We have good communication. They helped me set goals for recovery such as a good amount of running by November, which I achieved. I do racing in my head all the time. When I'm out biking, I do it frequently. I transform myself. I see and hear the crowd, the announcer, other runners I know, meet directors, etc. I see it all. I see myself going out fast, running in the pack, hurting like in a race, see the finish line, see myself winning. I've always seen myself winning.

"When I'm at my best physically, I always feel like I can win. In talking to other people, I don't sense that in most of them. They are finding excuses. They're already talking themselves out of doing well. I don't do that. When I'm training and I'm fit, I feel that I can win."

She is, of course, taking care of her legs. Low mileage, high quality, plenty of other exercise such as biking or swimming, and running on softer surfaces. No wasted miles. "Just working out with the team is so nice. Nothing else gives me such a feeling of energy. Before the surgeries, when I was healthy, it was like I wasn't even there. Workouts felt stale. I was running faster than ever but I wasn't enjoying it then like I do now. If nothing else, all this has helped my running mentally. If I can overcome this, I can take anything anybody throws at me."

A Visualization Program for Healing

Another process for dealing with injury involves visualizing the injury itself. Through mental imagery it is possible to alter the body's autonomic physiological responses. In other words, you can communicate with your body using imagery, suggestion, and language—exactly what we have been writing about in this book. When you use your imagination, mental pictures, and suggestion, you can make your body respond.

These techniques have been widely taught and practiced by several physicians in the United States, among them Dr. David Bresler, the director of the UCLA Pain Control Unit and a prominent researcher into imagery, Dr. Norman Shealy in his Pain Rehabilitation Center in Wisconsin, and Dr. Carl Simonton in the Fort Worth Cancer Clinic. Just as mental imagery can produce a state of relaxation, mental images can facilitate and enhance the speed and effectiveness of the healing process.

Again, you must enter as deep a state of relaxation as possible. Then create an image in your mind's eye of what you want your body to do with the injured area. The image may be highly technical, or simple and imaginative. Perhaps you imagine the stress fracture site mending, the bone knitting together, the blood cells surrounding the site, bringing new oxygen, replenishing and energizing the injury, and all the "bad blood" and wastes being removed. A fanciful example might be visualizing rays of golden or white light surrounding the injury site, bringing warmth and healing, energizing the site and your whole body. It is most important that the healing image feels good to you and has personal significance.

The following is an adaptation of a visualization process described by Dennis T. Jaffe, Ph.D., in his excellent book, *Healing from Within,* (Knopf, 1980).*

"Let your attention wander to the particular bodily part that is a source of discomfort or illness, or does not function properly. Direct all your thoughts to this selected area and allow yourself to experience what it feels like right now. After a moment, allow a picture related to that region to enter your mind. It may be a detailed representation of what you think that part looks like internally. Or it could be more fanciful, reflecting how that bodily region feels to you. Keep your attention there until you are satisfied with the picture you've created.

"Now begin to visualize a process taking place within your image, making that part of your body function better, or start healing. You might envision energy flowing into it. Let your imagination judge its appropriateness. A strong healing image could actually cause you to feel better right away.

"Next, spend five or ten minutes holding that picture in your mind, using it as a focusing thought for a period of meditation. If you find your mind wandering, gently return it to your healing image. However, if your picture starts changing, simply let it happen, watching the transformation occur.

*From HEALING FROM WITHIN, by Dennis T. Jaffe, Copyright © 1980 by Dennis T. Jaffe. Reprinted by permission of Alfred A. Knopf, Inc.

"Over the ensuing weeks, focus on your healing image for a few minutes twice a day, as part of your regular meditation or relaxation process. Many individuals discover that their images are always with them in the background. From time to time during the day, they find themselves spontaneously focusing upon their healing image, allowing it to remain there for a few moments. While your conscious imagery work will take only a few minutes each day, your unconscious and your body will spend nearly all the time on the healing process if you do not distract them with excessive stress or external demands."

Think of the marked contrast between this use of imagery and your usual response to pain or illness. Too often, you probably clench your muscles, become angry, or desperately try to ignore the discomfort, hoping that aspirin or a more potent analgesic will ease the pain. Such a response makes you even more tense, creating further obstacles for your body to contend with. But in a healing visualization, you directly confront and assault the dysfunction within you by mobilizing the positive forces that can aid in the healing. Instead of passively or naively working against yourself, you actively stimulate whatever latent powers of healing lie within. You have nothing to lose and much to gain by joining in this experiment in self-healing.

Physicians treat our bodies, but the body must heal and repair itself. Through imagination and relaxation, our natural healing processes can be developed and maintained. For specific examples and clarification, see Jaffe's book.

Talking to Your Body Parts

Another technique, emphasized by Neurolinguistic Programing (NLP) pioneers John Grinder and Richard Bandler, involves talking to body parts. Talking to your body parts increases body awareness. When you feel discomfort, relax your body and mind and ask your tight legs or muscles what you can do to take care of them. By becoming aware of your body's needs, you will be more able to take care of physical problems that are hidden from your normal consciousness.

This dialogue is an effective way of exploring unconscious body messages and meanings of pain and symptoms. A dialogue develops between your conscious and unconscious. Information is revealed in an intimate and shared conversation with the inner self.

Begin in a deeply relaxed state. Imagine the pain or discomfort taking human form and having its own separate voice. Start to create a dialogue between the symptom or injured part and your conscious self. As you continue to practice this technique, a dialogue will develop quite automatically. In his book, *Healing from Within*, Dr. Jaffe gives relevant examples of such dialogues. His patients were surprised at what emerged when trying this method. He explains that the left brain or logical brain activity is diminished during this process, and communication with the inner self emerges. As an athlete using this process, you will uncover important information about yourself. In asking why a symptom or pain exists, there is always an answer that has relevance to your life. Often you will discover feelings that you were not facing or a source of anxiety or conflict. Jaffe found that the healing process improved rapidly after one realized that part of oneself had been denied, forgotten, ignored, or rejected.

One method that seems to help is talking to your inner "advisor" or "guide" during a visualization process. The visualization begins with a deep relaxation process such as described in chapter 4. After relaxing, imagine that you are in a place that you love very much, where you feel peaceful and at home. Create a vivid picture in your mind and imagine yourself there feeling, hearing, smelling, tasting, and seeing the place. This is a place where your mind has taken you and where you feel relaxed, safe, and open. Imagine yourself feeling calm, peaceful, and centered in this place. Then proceed to wait for someone or something to join you. Perhaps a wise person, relative, animal, plant, or light will appear. Whatever the form, this unconscious part of you will furnish you with important information about your body. If no one appears, you might ask yourself why you do not wish to communicate with that part of yourself.

After contacting your advisor, greet him or her or it and begin to talk in your imagination. Eventually your advisor will answer your questions and help you to know what you need to do to overcome your physical problems. Dialogues are usually simple, clear, direct, and explicit. Ask the part what it wants or needs and what it is avoiding. Sometimes your advisor will remove the symptom once you start to change your behavior. If you remain relaxed and receptive to this process, you will see that the inner dialogue is an important way to circumvent beliefs, expectations, and mental patterns that keep you "stuck."

By contacting this "inner healer," you will become more in harmony in your mind and body. Eventually you will begin to see changes in your behavior and become more relaxed and less anxious about yourself and others. You will start to feel better about yourself and your injury. We, as well as Jaffe, believe that this kind of self-exploration and self-care results in maximizing physical and mental health and well-being.

Pain Control Techniques for Injuries

One pain control technique that uses visualization is described by Jaffe as "glove anesthesia." This technique can be useful to you as an athlete when you are in acute pain from your injury, or can be used for any chronic athletic pain.

Guide yourself into a relaxed state. Imagine immersing your hand in ice water and continue doing that until your hand feels numb. Once you have created this numbness, place your hand on the part of your body in pain. Imagine the coldness moving from your hand to the painful area. Imagine the painful area becoming colder and colder and then numbing. Keep your hand on the area until the entire area has lost all sensation including pain. With practice, your discomfort will be eased more quickly.

Another method recommended by Jaffe is to visualize

the pain getting smaller and smaller. This method works because focusing attention on the pain focuses on the muscle tension. Imagine the muscle tissue surrounding the pain relaxing. When you center on the pain, you face it directly; you are not fearful or avoiding it. By confronting and acknowledging pain through relaxation rather than fear and anxiety, you release yourself from the intensity of the pain.

An excellent pain control technique comes from the work of Stephen Levine, a therapist who works with dying and terminally ill patients. The following pain meditation from Levine's book *Who Dies** (Anchor Books, 1982) can be a very effective visualization for reducing either acute or chronic athletic pain:

> Sit or lie down in a position you find comfortable. Allow yourself to settle into this position so that the whole body feels fully present where it sits or lies.
>
> Bring your attention to the area of sensation that has been uncomfortable.
>
> Let your attention come wholly to that area. Let the awareness be present, moment to moment, to receive the sensations generated there.
>
> Allow the discomfort to be felt.
>
> Moment to moment new sensations seem to arise.
>
> Does the flesh cramp against the pain? Feel how

*Courtesy of Stephen Levine in *Who Dies*, Anchor Books, New York, 1982.

the body tends to grasp it in a fist, tries to close it off.

Begin to allow the body to open all around the sensation.

Feel the tension and resistance that comes to wall off the sensation.

Don't push away the pain. Just let it be there. Feel how the body is clenched in resistance.

Feel how the body holds each new sensation.

Begin gradually to open that closedness around sensation. The least resistance can be so painful.

Open. Soften. All around the sensation.

Allow the fist, moment to moment, to open. To give space to the sensation.

Let go of the pain. Why hold on a moment longer?

Like grasping a burning ember, the flesh of the closed fist is seared in its holding. Open. Soften all around the sensation. Let the fist of resistance begin to loosen. To open.

The palm of that fist softening. The fingers beginning to loosen their grip. Opening. All around the sensation.

The fist loosening. Gradually opening. Moment to moment, letting go of the pain. Release the fear that surrounds it.

Notice any fear that has accumulated around the pain. Allow the fear to melt. Let tension dissolve, so that the sensations can softly radiate out as they will. Don't try to capture the pain. Let it float free. No longer held in the grasp of resistance. Softening. Opening all around the sensation. The fist opening. The fingers, one by one, loosening their grip.

The sensation no longer encapsulated in resistance. Opening.

Let the pain soften. Let the pain be. Let go of the resistance that tries to smother the experience.

Allow each sensation to come fully into consciousness. No holding. No pushing away. The pain beginning to float free in the body.

All grasping relinquished. Just awareness and sensation meeting moment to moment. Received gently by the softening flesh.

The fist opened into a soft, spacious palm. The fingers loose. The fist dissolved back into the soft, open flesh. No tension. No holding.

Let the body be soft and open. Let the sensation float free. Easy. Gently.

Softening, opening all around the pain.

Just sensation. Floating free in the soft, open body.

This pain meditation, when said daily, will begin to create a mental environment that will loosen your mind's grip on the pain and your avoidance. The area around the pain and your mental reaction to that pain will begin to relax, facilitating healing and removing your active resistance to it. After removing resistance, your mind can focus on healing and more positive images.

In all of these techniques, you choose how you wish

to cope with your injury or pain. We are not advocating that you perform with pain. These methods are for you to use in managing and dealing with athletic and injury pain when you need relief.

Each technique centers around our general mental training program of positive self-thoughts and visualizations. It is important that you send energy, light, and love to your injured or painful body part and that you regard it as a friend to be helped and healed rather than an enemy to be resented or feared. When you wish to eliminate the problem, it helps to tell the body part it is loved and that you wish for it to be healed so it can assist you in your athletic performance.

Simple affirmations such as "I am healthy;" "I am healing rapidly;" "I am healed;" "My body is repairing itself perfectly;" will allow your mind to assist rapid recovery and the healing process your body is attempting. Seeing yourself healed and healthy is the first step on your journey to recovery.

I AM READY AND
CONCENTRATING ON THE BALL.

CHAPTER TEN

Keeping a Mental Training Log

If you continue to do what you have always done, you will continue to get what you have always gotten.

Gary Koyen

Just as athletes keep track of their physical training and condition, so should they keep a mental training log. As we have said throughout this book, this is a training—something done everyday, something monitored and analyzed so the athlete becomes aware of patterns and can make changes and improvements. We all have thought processes that benefit and support us in a multitude of ways, and we also have beliefs and habits that tend to limit us. Most of the time we are not aware of what these are or of how they help or hinder us.

Now that you have a working knowledge of this comprehensive mental training program, you can be much more aware of your mental process as you physically train and compete in your sport. With this final and extremely important step in our program, you have more control over your patterns of thought and belief as you progress.

The Process

A mental training log is a diary kept after each significant workout and each competition. It is a written account of your emotional/intellectual process as you warm up, perform, and finish your physical activity. It contains your inner thoughts and pictures, your fears and emotional strengths. It is the story of how you as an athlete, and ultimately as a person, think, react, process, and support your physical performance and competence.

For example: You are a figure skater entering your first competition of the year. You are not too sure of the ice or the judges and you have not competed since last winter. You also know that last year's state champion is competing just after you. You stand at the edge waiting to hear your name, waiting to step onto the ice. What is happening in your head? Are you breathing? Is your coach talking to you, giving you some last instructions? Do you hear the words? How do they make you feel?

As you step down and begin to glide across the ice, how does your body feel in general? Are you relaxed and smooth, or are you tense and stiff? What is your reaction to your physical state of being? If you fall, what do you say to yourself? If you do your triple leap perfectly, what is your inner voice saying? While you are competing, focus on your performance. When you finish, become aware as much as possible of the inner words, concepts, and feelings that guided you to do well or to do less than your best.

Within twenty-four hours, write this mental awareness down. Write it down fully, from beginning to end, good and bad. Be as clear and honest as you can, noting as many internal words and beliefs as you remember. When you stepped onto the ice, you may remember that you were thinking "well, here we go . . . let's have fun . . . you know you're ready," and when you saw the state champion standing at the edge just as you went into the approach of your final jump, a little voice may have said, "I don't think I'll ever be good enough to beat her," or maybe, "boy, I have been right on this whole routine; she will have to work hard to beat me." When you feel you have written down everything you can remember, read it over once, noticing the positive things and the negative things. Remember what you were doing when you were being positive and let go of the negative things for the time being.

Continue to keep this log for at least three weeks of your physical training and competition without paying too much attention to it other than to make your entries. At the end of three weeks, go back to the beginning (this is a good time to have your coach with you) and read through your mental process for those last three weeks. Do you notice any patterns? As you read, ask yourself these key questions:

- What were the positive thoughts and feelings I had and what did they do for me?
- What were the negative thoughts, beliefs and feelings I had and how did they hinder me?
- Did I overcome these negative thoughts? If so, how?

Begin to analyze each performance, each entry, for similarities, differences, strengths and weaknesses. Find out what you do in your mind that helps you perform at your peak. Become aware of the mental and emotional beliefs, reactions, and words that limit your performance. Become aware of the times you feel the most powerful and when you feel powerless, frustrated, and out of control. Note any patterns that appear during this three-week log.

MENTAL TRAINING LOG

Event: ______________________ Date: ______________

Finishing Place/Score: ____________ My Goal: _______

General Feelings, Successes, Doubts:

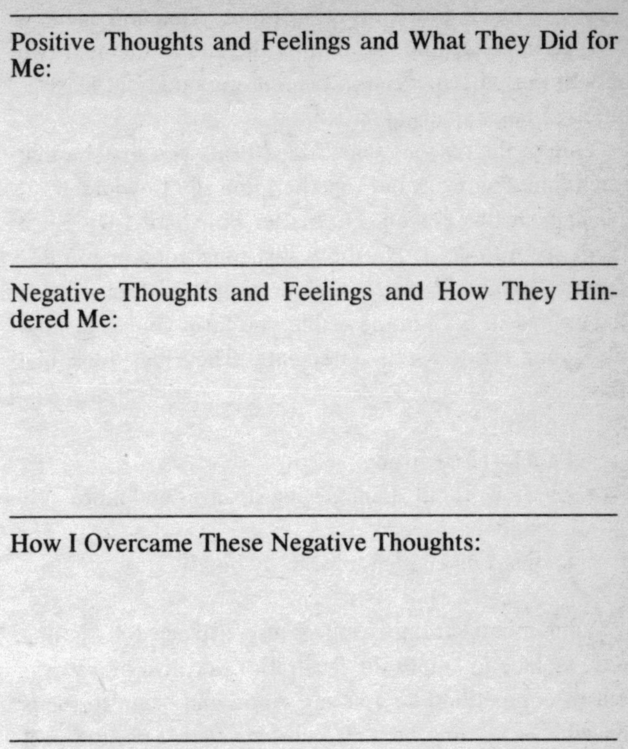

Positive Thoughts and Feelings and What They Did for Me:

Negative Thoughts and Feelings and How They Hindered Me:

How I Overcame These Negative Thoughts:

Keeping a journal or log after each important workout and each competition will begin to show you not only your strengths and weaknesses but help you form your goals. If, during your last two weeks of workouts, your best buddy has beaten you each time, your goal for the next two months might look like this, "I want to beat my buddy at least every other workout. This will mean a change in my attitude so that by the end of the next two month period I succeed in beating my buddy at least as often as he or she beats me."

One of the reasons your friend beats you may be that each time you work out together, you say to yourself: "I never beat this person. No matter how hard I try I just can't seem to do it. He/she is just too strong or too fast for me." You will notice such a thought pattern in your log entries. It is from these that you form your goals and also your positive self-statements. They may look like this:

- I am fast and strong.
- Every workout, I am getting stronger and more confident.
- I am strong enough to beat my buddy.

Your mental training log is also a place for "letting go," a place to empty the frustrations or joys of a workout or competition so you can go on and begin to focus on what is coming next. It will help you leave the past behind and clear the way for learning and positive input. A mental log will highlight patterns, enabling you to make use of the positive processes that work for you and change those negative and limiting patterns that keep you from achieving your peak athletic performance.

Awareness is curative.

Tim Gallway

CHAPTER ELEVEN

Designing a Program for Peak Performance

In the previous chapters we have led you through the steps of our Mental Training for Peak Performance program. This chapter highlights five athletes in five different sports: a high school basketball player, a tennis player, an 800/1500-meter runner, a triathlete, and a golfer. Goals and affirmations are developed for each athlete, and a visualization is included for each. These are examples and outlines of how we developed and organized specific programs aimed at the defined goals of each of these athletes. These outlines can be used as models for programs you design for your athletic or life goals.

MY FORM IS SMOOTH AND RHYTHMIC

Basketball

Mark Snow is a highly skilled high school basketball player. He has had the usual problems of nervousness and butterflies before a game or a tryout. He wanted to learn ways of feeling calm, relaxed, and happy and to improve his mood. When he was nervous, he lacked confidence and started missing shots in games and in practice. When he was properly "psyched," he played well and aggressively, shooting with more accuracy. In basketball, it is important to be aggressive and hustling one minute and calm, cool, and collected the next. When a player shoots a free throw, calmness and centeredness is crucial. Young players often have difficulty making this transition.

When working with Mark, we worked on goals and affirmations and led him through a guided visualization each session. He read his affirmations each morning and every night. The visualizations often included shooting jumpshots, lay-ups, and free throws, defensive positioning and general execution—centered around feelings of calm, control, energy, and strength when appropriate.

At one point Mark was injured with a chipped and sprained ankle. His visualizations and goals then focused on weight lifting, physical therapy, and healing. Progressive relaxation was always included in his visualizations. He also learned how to cope when a coach gave him a bad time or "rode" him. We worked with him on learning to hear criticism, not taking it personally, and keeping his concentration and focus. We also spent time teaching him the philosophy and ideas described in this book.

GOALS AND AFFIRMATIONS

His goals currently center around some common problems and concerns of both male and female basketball players at the high school level. These are his goals:

Short-Term

1. Become proficient at dribbling with my left hand (he is right-handed) so I can work well from my left side as well as my right.
2. Have the correct follow-through on all shots.

Intermediate

1. Be able to outscore any opponent I guard. Be better defensively than they are offensively.
2. Never allow an opponent to get past me on rebounds. In defensive guarding, screen them out and prevent them from getting the rebound.

Long-Term

1. Be able to see the coach's point of view. Be able to accept constructive criticism and not take it personally. Know the coach is trying to help me become the best player I can be.

2. To be a starter.
3. Make all-district.
4. Make all-state.
5. Get scholarship to play college basketball.

These are his affirmations:

Short-term

1. a. I dribble well with my left hand.
   b. I dribble smoothly and easily with my left hand.
   c. I enjoy dribbling with my left hand.
2. a. I follow through corectly on all my shots.
   b. I have good follow-through.
   c. I have good form on my shots.

Intermediate

1. a. I outscore the man I am guarding.
   b. I am a good defensive player.
   c. I am a high scorer.
   d. I shoot well and consistently.
   e. I am a strong and accurate shooter.
2. a. I am an excellent rebounder.
   b. I enjoy getting rebounds.

c. I screen out my opponent and prevent him from getting the rebound.
d. I enjoy defense and do it well.

Long-Term

1. a. The coach helps and supports me.
   b. I learn a lot from my coach's constructive feedback.
   c. I enjoy and appreciate the feedback my coach gives me and use it to my advantage.
   e. The coach is on my side and is for me.

2. a. I play a starting position.
   b. I am a starter.

3. a. I am on the all district team.
   b. I am an all district player.
   c. I make all district.

4. a. I am on the all state team.
   b. I make all state.
   c. I am a member of the all state team.

5. a. I get a scholarship to play college basketball.
   b. I am a college basketball player on scholarship.
   c. I play college basketball on a scholarship.

GENERAL AFFIRMATIONS FOR BASKETBALL

- I am in control of my emotions when I play.
- I am relaxed, ready, and alert.

- I am a strong and confident player.
- I am an aggressive, ethical player.
- I am a confident athlete.
- I am as good as anyone on the court today/tonight.
- I like myself and my abilities.
- I trust myself and am open to feedback from others.
- I am totally relaxed and focused.
- I have excellent concentration.
- I am calm, cool, and collected while playing.
- I am totally focused and within myself when shooting a free throw.
- I support and encourage my teammates.
- All the team members support one another.
- I am easily able to go from an intense playing situation to a calm state for free throw shooting.
- I am aware of everything happening around me in a game.
- I am quick and fast.
- I have a fast reaction time.
- I am an excellent dribbler.

GUIDED VISUALIZATION FOR BASKETBALL

(Use a progressive relaxation technique from chap. 4 before beginning this visualization.)

Imagine yourself arriving at the gym . . . feel the usual feelings of slight nervousness . . . excitement . . . anticipation. See the court, your fellow players, the coach . . . feel the excitement in the air and listen to the crowd.

You begin to warm up on the court . . . dribbling . . . running . . . shooting . . . the team is going through their warm-up drills . . . you enjoy the movement and anticipate the beginning of the game . . . you feed the ball to another player . . . you receive the ball . . . feel it in your hands and shoot again . . . see yourself dribbling with control, using both hands proficiently and well . . . you quickly think of your affirmations . . . you dribble . . . make a jump shot perfectly . . . feel your body following through correctly and perfectly . . . you again get the ball . . . dribble . . . leap up for a well placed layup . . . feel the shot in your body . . . the ball rolling off your wrist and index finger in the proper way. . . . You see the ball go into the hoop. . . .

You finish your warm-up . . . hear the instructions . . . you trust your teammates . . . everyone knows his position and how to play his best . . . the game begins . . . you move . . . run . . . pivot . . . run again . . . jockeying for position . . . staying with your man . . . you get the ball . . . you feed it perfectly to another teammate . . . you again get the ball . . . begin to dribble . . . execute the perfect layup for two points . . . you are playing very well . . . you feel strong, quick, light. . . .

See yourself playing . . . feel your body relaxed and alert . . . always ready for the next shot . . . you are totally focused. . . . "I have good focus and concentration . . . I am a calm, cool and collected player. . . ." It is easy for you tonight . . . you feel good and strong . . . you go after a rebound . . . you keep the ball away from your opponent . . . back and forth you move . . . to your basket . . . to the opponent's basket . . . guarding . . . jumping . . . scoring . . . passing . . . you are good and quick . . . you are defending well . . . moving smoothly . . . you continue to successfully screen out your opponent . . . you are fouled. . . .

Imagine yourself standing at the free-throw line waiting for the ball . . . you visualize your shot . . . perfectly correctly . . . you take a deep breath as you catch the ball and stand quietly . . . feel the ball in your hands . . . hear the sound as you bounce it in front of you . . . you look up at the rim. . . . breathe . . . and shoot, watching, concentrating on the front of the rim . . . the ball swishes in . . . perfectly . . . beautifully . . . just the way you wanted it . . . the game continues and you are moving again . . . you calmly and easily sink each shot you attempt . . . you remember with a smile, "I am aware and alert . . . I notice everything around me . . . I am focused and aware."

You are totally focused and immersed in the game as you play . . . moment by moment . . . always in the present . . . letting go of any mistakes you make . . . you are in the now . . . you play on, perfectly and in control until the final buzzer . . . your teammates encourage and support each other

...you are a team...."I love to play this game...I am a calm, controlled and powerful player..." It was a good game...you played your best and you feel great....

Let the illusion of the game slowly slip away... become aware of your body sitting in the chair or lying on the floor...breathe in...exhale...feel your easy effortless breathing...remember your feelings of calm and controlled playing...knowing that you hit your shots perfectly...you are an important part of the team...feel the pride, confidence, and pleasure of a game well played....When I count to three, you may open your eyes, feeling relaxed, confident, invigorated and refreshed...one...two...three....

Triathlon

Shelley Briggs is a 31-year-old triathlete. She has run since 1978 and has completed eleven marathons and two 50Ks. She races distances from 800 meters to a marathon. She competes in cross-country ski marathons in the winter and bicycle races throughout the year. She has completed ten 100-mile century races and two 200-mile double centuries. She has been a competitor in various sports most of her life. She, like many other women athletes her age, has a full time job and is married. Her husband, Steve, competes in the same sports. They often win their age divisions and sometimes win or place second or third in the overall competition in triathlons and bike races.

For those readers not familiar with the triathlon, we interviewed Shelley for a synopsis of the psychological aspects of a triathlon competition. Shelley's goals and affirmations reflect common concerns of triathletes. Mental toughness is needed at certain key points in the competition. To some, the swimming at a hard pace is the most difficult because of fear of cramps, tiring, and sinking if one gets too exhausted. It is important to stay calm, to reach with the arms, and to pull as hard as possible. It is important to get away from other swimmers, since they tend to swim on top of you, and there is much thrashing about at the beginning of a crowded race. "I was terrified at the beginning of my first triathlon. People were swimming on top of me, kicking me, hitting me. I was so panic stricken, I started hitting and kicking them to knock them off of me. You have to fight for your own space. I started to turn around and go back and then remembered I'd been carboloading and eating all week for this race. I thought, I've eaten too much! I can't stop now! This has been my goal for the whole year! So I turned around and kept on swimming. I was rattled and scared to death and I kept on going." The cold of the water can also be a problem. Although feeling numb, the swimmer must focus on his or her stroke and keeping a fast rhythm and pace.

In the biking section of the race, the legs, back, and neck get tired, and the triathlete must focus on relaxation, pace, and staying as low as possible on the bike.

Drafting behind another biker is prohibited in triathlon competition. Often one athlete will team up on the ride with another to keep each other going. Head winds are also a problem. Telling oneself that everyone else is battling the wind helps psychologically.

The running section is basically the same as any foot race. Two-thirds of the way through, no matter what the distance, the athlete begins to tire. Whenever runners "hit the wall," they do well to think about their legs being light and fast, that they are almost finished, and perhaps reflect on how much they have already accomplished. Staying with the positives and positive self-talk for encouragement and support helps the athlete maintain focus and control.

GOALS AND AFFIRMATIONS

These are Shelley's goals for the year:

Overall Triathlon Goals

1. To compete in the Iron Man triathlon.

2. To improve present PR in all three events.

3. To participate in two half-Iron Man events (1.2 mile swim, 56 mile bike ride, 13.1 mile race) and one or two events of standard triathlon distance (swim 1.5K (.93 miles), bike 40K (24.8 miles), run 10K (6.2 miles).

4. To qualify for nationals.

Specific Swim Goals

1. Push self at all times and not let up.
2. Swim as hard as I can all the way.
3. Let go of being afraid of getting too tired while swimming.

Specific Biking Goals

1. Keep spinning smooth and fast, never pushing hard gears.
2. Stay at 20 MPH or faster.
3. Keep cadence between 80-100 turns/minute.
4. After 15 miles in a 20-mile race, be sure cadence is 90-100 so legs are loosened up for running.

Specific Running Goals

1. At mile 9.7 in a 13.1 mile race, begin pushing self.
2. Push through tiredness.
3. Say affirmations for the half marathon starting at mile 8.
4. For a 10K, push hard from mile 3.5 to mile 5.
5. Finish fast and hard at end.
6. Sprint last 400 meters.

Overall Affirmations

1. a. I am accepted in the Iron Man competition.
   b. I compete in the Iron Man Triathlon in Hawaii.
   c. I finish the Iron Man competition.

2. a. I improve my present PR in all three events.
   b. I swim 32:50 or faster in the 1-mile swim.
   c. I bike 2:57 or faster in the 56-mile bike ride.
   d. I run 1:35 or faster in the half marathon.
   e. I am a tough competitor.

3. a. I compete in two half-marathon triathlons this year.
   b. I compete in two standard triathlons this year.

4. a. I qualify for the national triathlon championship.
   b. I compete well in the national triathlon championships.
   c. I place in the top five in the national triathlon championships.

Specific Swimming Affirmations

1. a. I push myself hard while swimming.
   b. I enjoy pushing myself in the swimming section.
   c. I am an excellent competitor in the swim.

2. a. I am strong and fast in the swim.
   b. I swim as hard as I can.
   c. It feels good to swim hard.

3. a. I am free of fear while swimming.
   b. I am relaxed and confident while swimming.
   c. I am confident and in control when I swim hard.

Specific Biking Affirmations

1. a. I keep my wheels spinning smoothly and fast.
   b. Spin fast and smooth.
   c. It is easy for me to keep spinning smoothly and quickly.

2. a. I am comfortable at 20 MPH.
   b. I ride consistently at 20 MPH or faster.
   c. I keep my speed at 20 MPH or faster.

3. a. I keep my cadence between 80-100 turns/minute.
   b. Keeping my cadence between 80-100 turns/minute is easy for me.
   c. My legs are strong and fast at 80-100 turns/minute.

4. a. At 15 miles of a 20-mile race, I easily increase my cadence to 90-100.
   b. My legs are relaxed and loose.

c. My legs are relaxed and loose during the last quarter of the bike race.
d. I enjoy increasing my cadence during the end of the bike race.

Specific Running Affirmations

1. a. I begin pushing hard at mile 9 or 10 in the half-marathon.
   b. I enjoy this part of the race.
   c. It feels good to push myself toward the end of the race.

2. a. I easily push through tiredness.
   b. The race will be over soon and I am going great.
   c. I've worked hard for this and I am confident of my ability and strength.
   d. Keep on pushing, I am almost finished.

3. a. I am a strong and fast runner.
   b. I am fit and fast.
   c. I am a tough competitor.
   d. I am an excellent runner and this is a piece of cake.

4. a. I enjoy pushing hard from mile 3.5 to mile 5 of a 10K race.
   b. 3.5 to 5 miles is the best part of my 10K race.
   c. I accelerate easily from 3.5 to 5 miles in the 10K race.

5. a. I am a fast finisher and have a good kick.
   b. I finish hard and fast.
   c. The last half-mile, I run hard andstrong.

6. a. I have plenty of energy and spring the last 400 meters.
   b. I am a good sprinter.
   c. I enjoy the last 400 meters and love sprinting at the end.
   d. I am an excellent triathlete.

GUIDED VISUALIZATION FOR THE TRIATHLON

(Begin with a progressive relaxation from chap. 4)

See yourself arriving at the triathlon course . . . noticing the people, the environment . . . you are getting ready for the swim . . . you are in your suit and goggles . . . number written on your leg or arm . . . people are milling around, engrossed in their own thoughts . . . listen to the sounds and feel the energy around you and within you. You do your warm-up routine . . . the bike is ready, the running shoes are waiting . . . let them go from your mind . . . you begin to say your swimming affirmations to yourself . . . relax . . . remember some of your goals . . . excelling in the swim . . . pushing yourself hard . . . being free of fear . . . swimming as hard and fast as you can. . . .

You line up . . . feeling the excitement in your body . . . hearing the instructions . . . watching the water . . . waiting . . . the gun goes off. . . . You run to the water and charge in feeling the coldness on your skin . . . people are all around you . . . you remain calm, swimming with your arms pulling hard toward you . . . you remind yourself to keep pushing . . . you focus on your form and your stroke . . . moving for a good position out of the crowd . . . picking up your pace as you go . . . pushing hard . . . feeling relaxed and ready . . . stroking evenly and in control . . . pulling the water toward you. "I am a strong, smooth and powerful swimmer. . . ." You make the halfway point . . . swimming hard, fast, powerfully through the water . . . seeing the shore . . . feeling yourself slicing through the water smoothly . . . closer and closer . . . you can hear your rhythmic splashing as your arms move powerfully . . . stroking . . . pulling . . . you swim harder, knowing you are almost finished . . . you will soon be out of the water . . . you are doing a good job . . . you have pushed hard all the way.

You reach the shore . . . run to the change area and get into your clothes as quickly as you can . . . you feel the pull of the material on your wet skin . . . you are focused and in control as you jump on your bicycle and take off . . . pedaling furiously . . . establishing good speed. . . . "That was fast . . . great job . . . got that done perfectly. . . ." . . . you settle into the bicycle rhythm, pedaling smoothly . . . your hands and feet begin to warm up slowly . . . you are

. . . fast and smooth . . . you spin powerfully with your legs . . . pedaling hardthe bicycle to a comfortable position . . . riding confidently next er biker. You begin to talk . . . nice way to keep yourself going . . . you folled . . . your cadence is good, just where you want it to be . . . you spin powerfully, maintaining your ninety turns/minute . . . your wheels are spinning faster . . . easier gears . . . you feel good . . . leaning into the hills . . . using control on the down-grade . . . eating some bananas, drinking water, refreshing yourself with some needed carbos . . . feeling a little tiredness and feeling good at the same time.

Remember your affirmations and goals for this biking section . . . spinning smooth and fast . . . working hard . . . feeling good . . . almost finished . . . the ground seems to be flying by now . . . you are leaving it all behind you as you come closer and closer to the finish. . . . Thoughts of running begin to enter your mind . . . you notice them and then let them go as you focus on a hard "sprint" to the finish. . . .

You ride over to your assigned spot, put your bike in its proper place, and quickly put on your running shoes . . . lacing each with speed and control . . . you take off running . . . aaahhhh, your legs feel good, they are loose and warm and ready to go . . . you begin to loosen up all over . . . warming up . . . breathing hard and deeply . . . your body settles into its rhythm . . . you feel very good

. . . this is the easy part for you . . . become aware of the pavement under your feet and the sound your strides make. . . . "I am a powerful runner . . . this is my strongest event . . . I run hard and with ease for the next three miles."

Begin to push yourself after three miles . . . picking up the pace . . . you say your affirmations . . . you see the six-mile mark up ahead . . . you are passing some other runners now . . . in complete control . . . you push . . . surging . . . passing . . . accelerating . . . beginning to sprint the last 400 meters . . . passing more runners . . . taking them all by surprise . . . you cross the finish line . . . one of the first across the line . . . you gasp for breath . . . sides heaving . . . breathing hard . . . tired . . . exhilarated . . . excited . . . joyful . . . pleased. . . .

Feel the euphoria rising in your body . . . the happiness, the contentment . . . you know you have won . . . you have done your best . . . you have reached your goals . . . experience it all in your body . . . thanking your body for all it has given you today . . . let it all flow through your entire body . . . in every blood vessel and every cell . . . feel the pride, the confidence, the sense of accomplishment . . . hear the crowd . . . your friends and those you don't know . . . experience it all.

Let the vision slip away . . . inhale . . . exhale . . . inhale . . . exhale . . . feel your body in the chair or on the floor . . . experience again the feelings of completion, happiness and contentment from doing your best triathlon . . . when I count to three, you will open your eyes feeling refreshed, invigorated and confident . . . one . . . two . . . three. . . .

Track: 800/1500 Meters

Ranza Clark is a 23-year-old, national-class, middle distance runner from Canada. She competed for four years at the University of Oregon on the team with Leann Warren, Claudette Groenendaal, and Kathy Hayes. Her PR's are 2:01.7 in the 800 and 4:07.5 in the 1500, and she intends to compete for several more years. She ran in the 1984 Olympics on the Canadian team and qualified to the semifinals in the 800. She is an excellent runner who will continue to improve her times as she competes at the national and international level.

Ranza's response to her first Olympics was a common one. "I was shocked and pleased to be selected for the Canadian team. My own standards for making the team were a 2:00 flat or faster and here I was "bang" on the team. I wasn't really mentally prepared for the idea, though I was running really well. When in L.A., during workouts, I started looking at the other athletes, looking at the Romanian women who appeared so really strong and here I was. I think it would be really easy to just get psyched out looking at the body types of these women because they're so muscular and strong looking. They all run well under two minutes.

"I know I was just scared and worried. I wanted to do

really well but I couldn't get it to be a great big bang... everything's going to happen now! There was a lot of pressure from other people telling you, 'This is the greatest goal of your life.'

"I was scared to go out too fast in the first races. I got to the semifinal and I felt better. There were some physical problems. There were elbows and jostling. I was tripped twice, and the second time I nearly went down completely. It blew my whole concentration. I ended up running slower in the Olympics than I have in collegiate meets in Eugene. If I'd been better prepared mentally and physically, I'd have run a lot better at the Olympics. I don't think I've ever been lower on my confidence level.

"Once the Olympics were over, I went to Europe. I wanted to race more. It's nice to race in Europe. You know you'll get a lot of races to run and there is never any pressure on you. I felt a lot better when I got over there. You're completely on your own and running for yourself. It's so different. You don't have to worry about running for a team. You're running for yourself, not living up to someone else's expectations. I ran my 4:07.5 (1500 meters) PR in Europe. I was very confident and had good concentration. I knew that was the answer. In the race I was much more aggressive and I felt confident and in complete control."

GOALS AND AFFIRMATIONS

With that important year behind her, Ranza put together her program for the next year aimed at keeping her confidence and improving her PR.

Short-Term Goals

1. To feel OK about missing training when sick or injured.
2. To run 2:01 or faster in the 800 meters.

Intermediate

1. To increase basic leg speed.
2. To improve my 800 PR through racing in next six months.

Long-Term Goals

1. To win the Canadian Championship in both the 800 and 1500 meters.
2. To win a gold medal in the 800 or 1500 meters in my next big international competition in 1986.

Short-Term Affirmations

1. a. I heal quickly.
   b. I am fit and fast.
   c. It is OK to take time off from running to heal.

d. My body is healthy and rested.
e. I run even better after time off to heal.
f. I am well rested and ready to run well.

2. a. I run a 2:01 or faster.
   b. I run under a 2:01.
   d. I am in excellent shape.
   d. Lifting weights makes me stronger.

Intermediate Affirmations

1. a. I have great speed in my legs.
   b. Speed work is fun and I enjoy it.
   c. Doing speed work makes me explosive and fast.
   d. I have a good kick.
   e. I reach my full speed potential.

2. a. I run a PR in the 800 in the next six months.
   b. I break 2:00 in the 800.
   c. I run the 800 in 2:00 or faster.

Long-Term Affirmations

1. a. I win the 1985 Canadian Championships in the 1500 meters.
   b. I win the 1985 Canadian Championships in the 800 meters.
   c. I am a gold medalist at the 1985 Canadian Championships in August.

2. a. I win my next international competition in 1986 in the 1500 meters.

b. I win my next international competition in 1986 in the 800 meters.

GENERAL AFFIRMATIONS FOR 800/1500 METERS

Health and Body

- I am lean and fast.
- I am all muscle strength.
- I am a strong and powerful runner.
- I am healthy and fit.

Training

- I love the feeling of completing a difficult, strenuous workout.
- A good workout is always worth the effort.
- Even though I may be tired, the second half of the workout goes quickly and I perform well.

Competition

- I get psyched up and excited about racing.
- I am ready to burst forth at the line.
- I enjoy the "soreness" of pushing hard and giving everything while racing.
- I have a strong kick.

Injury

- My body regenerates quickly.
- Time off from running is constructive.

- My body heals quickly.
- I am excited about running and competing again.
- I run well, even better, after time off to heal.
- I am running pain free.

GUIDED VISUALIZATION FOR THE 800 METERS

(Use one of the progressive relaxations in chap. 4 before this and the next visualization.)

See yourself arriving at the track where you will be competing, wearing your uniform and your sweats. As you get out of the car, your mind is on the race. Notice the environment . . . what the weather is like . . . the sun, the clouds . . . whatever you can see. Notice the other runners and feel yourself to be calm, confident and relaxed . . . really feeling good. You are anticipating running . . . looking forward to your race . . . you have a deep, calm feeling inside, knowing that you are very well prepared . . . you have been doing your training and you are ready. See yourself doing your normal warm-up routine . . . imagine yourself doing your stretches and your warm-up sequence that gets you ready for your race . . . stretches, strides, warm-up jogs. Visualize yourself going through all the motions of your warm-up routine. After you have completed your warm-ups, see yourself taking off your sweats, doing your final stretches . . . your final strides . . . and lining up at the starting line for the 800-meter race you are about to run.

Hear the starter giving you the instructions . . . you notice your opponents and you recognize some of them . . . you know their strengths and weaknesses . . . feel yourself very relaxed, yet excited and anticipating this race. You can feel the adrenalin flowing in your body, and you are relaxed . . . your muscles are ready to go. You are calm and yet alert, knowing you will be ready to take off when you hear the gun and that you are ready for this race. You have been looking forward to it for a long time.

As you stand at the starting line, you can feel the familiar pounding of your heart . . . that familiar excitement that courses through your body before any race. Know that you are there to run and that you will run very well. You have been anticipating this race and looking forward to it, and you will enjoy it thoroughly. The gun sounds and you take off . . . everyone is racing and jockeying for position . . . the pack settles into a fast comfortable pace and you have a good position in the pack. Make sure to take your time . . . keeping relaxed and fluid . . . fast and relaxed . . . stay with the people you want to stay with . . . be in the position you want to be in at the beginning of the race. You are watching the other people around you out of the corner of your eye . . . keeping track of where they are . . . knowing that you are running a strong, controlled race. Your stride is smooth . . . you are centered and balanced and feel comfortable . . . you are enjoying this race very much. You love the feeling of competition . . . coming around the curve . . . you love to lean into the curves . . . feel that power and energy surging through your body.

You are finishing the first lap. You know your strategy . . . you continue to implement this strategy . . . you start surging, moving ahead, passing people . . . you start your kick. It feels as if you're going into overdrive . . . you are picking it up. You feel the intensity in the race . . . you feel the excitement . . . you feel the power in your body . . . you feel the control in your body . . . you are running and running. You are concentrating on this third 200 meters. You relax and run hard, mentally preparing for the final 200 of the race. You get in position . . . this last stretch is important. You are ready and confident. You stride out, passing the 600 meter point. You start the final 200 meters, go into the curve, running fast and relaxed . . . striding, arms pumping powerfully . . . blasting off the final curve into the home stretch. You're a sprinter now . . . moving powerfully down the straightaway. You have good form and you are keeping that form . . . you feel like you're floating . . . very fast . . . you are just flying along and you are passing the people you want to pass. You can feel the energy surging through your body . . . feel the control . . . feel the power . . . your legs and your arms are pumping and moving and you feel good.

You're coming down the final 50 meters, picking it up even more now, and you and your competitor are shoulder to shoulder. You dig deep inside yourself for that extra reserve you have been saving and turn it on. You move by this last competitor. You maintain your speed and form . . . taking strong, powerful strides, always smooth and confident. You feel your body in perfect control and perfect form striding out and moving away. You look up and see the finish line and tape. You fly toward the line and you feel the tape hit your chest and know that you have won.

A feeling of euphoria and elation passes through your body. You know that you have done what you wanted to do. You know how strong you are and you have the joy of achieving your goal . . . the satisfaction and the completion of a job well done . . . you know you are strong mentally and physically, and you have the physical and psychological edge over your opponents. You have done your physical training and mental training and it has all paid off.

You come to a standstill . . . your sides are heaving . . . you are getting your breath. You have a feeling of complete satisfaction and joy. People are coming up to you and shaking your hand, slapping your back. They're happy for you too. Hear their voices full of excitement and listen to what they are saying.

Having caught your breath, you jog slowly, knowing the taste of victory and savoring it in this special moment of your life . . . this moment of total satisfaction when you have done your best. You thank your body . . . your legs, your lungs, and all your body parts for the excellent way they have helped you and served you. You jog around the track on your victory lap to the applause of your friends and people you don't even know who've enjoyed watching you race. You have achieved your goal.

Let go of the image and the feeling now and slowly begin to re-enter your present space. Reconnect with your physical world . . . the feel of the chair, the relaxation and heaviness of your arms and legs . . . gently move your toes and then your fingers . . . becoming aware of your breathing . . . inhale deeply . . . hold it . . . and exhale. You feel relaxed, and filled with new, quiet energy. When you are ready . . . open your eyes.

GUIDED VISUALIZATION FOR THE 1500 METERS

See yourself at the track where you will be competing, wearing your uniform and your sweats. Your mind is on the 1500 meter race. Notice the environment . . . what the weather is like . . . the sun, the clouds . . . whatever you can see. Notice the other runners and feel yourself to be calm, confident, and relaxed . . . really feeling good. You are anticipating running . . . looking forward to your race and have a deep, calm feeling inside knowing that you are very well prepared . . . you have been doing your training and you are ready. See yourself doing your normal warm-up routine . . . imagine yourself doing your stretches and the warm-up sequence that gets you ready for your race . . . stretches, strides, warm-up jogs. Visualize yourself going through all the motions of your warm-up routine.

After you have completed your warm-up, see yourself taking off your sweats, doing your final stretches . . . your final strides . . . and lining up at the starting line for the 1500 meter race you are about to run. Hear the starter giving you the instructions . . . you notice your opponents and weaknesses . . . feel yourself to be very relaxed, yet excited and anticipating this race. You can feel the adrenalin flowing in your body and you are relaxed . . . your muscles ready to go. You are calm and yet alert, knowing you will be ready to take off when you hear the gun and that you are ready for this race. You have been looking forward to it for a long time.

As you stand at the starting line, you can feel the familiar pounding of your heart . . . that familiar excitement that courses through your body before a race. Know that you are there to run and that you will run very well. The gun sounds and you take off . . . everyone is racing and jostling for position . . . the pack continues to change and move as you enter the first turn. Make sure to take your time . . . keeping relaxed and fluid . . . stay with the people you want to stay with . . . be in the position you want to be in at the beginning of the race. Someone bumps your shoulder . . . you keep your form and balance . . . you watch the other people around you out of the corner of your eye . . . keeping track of where they are. Your stride is smooth . . . you are centered and balanced and you feel comfortable . . . you are enjoying this race very much. You love the feeling of competition and feel the power and energy surging through your body as you lean into another curve. On this first lap, you feel yourself floating along easily in complete control.

You finish the first lap just cruising through and feeling very good. Starting on the second lap, you come out of the next curve and go down the back-stretch, maybe feeling the wind on your face a bit . . . knowing that your legs are strong. Though you are running into the wind, you have control and good form, tucking in behind someone perhaps leading . . . feeling perfectly comfortable and at ease within your body . . . still cruising feeling strong and running fast . . . going around the curves, down the stretch, finishing your second lap.

On the third lap, you begin to work hard and it feels good . . . think about your strategy . . . continue to implement your plans. Dig down inside yourself and know that if you push the pace a little, you are going to feel good . . . picking it up, just varying your pace slightly, you get another burst of energy. Knowing that all the runners are getting tired, you tell yourself that you are strong, you are in control, your form is good . . . you are hungry for this win . . . you want a good time. Feel yourself to be strong and in control. Pick it up a little, maybe passing, jockeying for another position in the pack . . . see where you want to be . . . watching the people around you . . . making sure you're in the right place . . . starting to make a few moves . . . getting around a few people that you want to get around . . . moving and knowing your strategy of this 1500 race.

Continue to execute your strategy as you approach the last lap. Feel your legs, know that they are there and they are strong. On your inhale, imagine bringing vital new tiredness that you might feel. Feel the renewed energy filling your body . . . your arms are strong; your legs are strong. Feel the air coming into your lungs . . . this is what you love . . . your body working, putting yourself against yourself . . . putting yourself against other runners. You love the competitive nature of this and you enjoy pushing yourself.

It is the bell lap. It is the 3/4 split. You know you have to pick it up now . . . to start your kick . . . you put on your surge . . . seeing yourself picking off person by person; getting in position on the straightway . . . passing whomever you want . . . see yourself leaning into the curve and running hard and feeling really good . . . coming off the curve, you attack the race . . . you let it all out. You know you have something left, and you shift into the last gear and feel yourself sprinting away. You are really picking it up and you are running just as fast as you can . . . flying down that last straightway. Feel your legs under you running and running and running. Feel the energy surging in your body. Pass that last person as if he or she were standing still. You can see the tape ahead . . . feel the tape on your chest as you burst across the finish line . . . enjoying that inner euphoria of having done your best . . . of feeling good . . . of being in control of your race.

Stopping . . . breathing heavily . . . breathing hard, trying to catch your breath . . . finally catching it . . . feeling good, having people touch you, pat you on the back, shake your hand. The exhilaration, the relief, the joy you feel when it's over. Slowly again you start to jog, to warm-down, to go around the track . . . your victory lap, slowly jogging, feeling a tremendous sense of accomplishment and completion. Listen to the applause . . . wave to your friends and know that you have run one of the best races in your life . . . feel the joy and excitement in your body . . . know that you were psychologically and physically prepared. Thank your body . . . your legs, your lungs and all your body parts . . . for the excellent way each has helped you and served you. You have achieved your goal.

Let go of the image and feeling now . . . slowly begin to re-enter your present space. Reconnect with your physical world . . . the feel of the chair

. . . the relaxation and heaviness of your arms and legs . . . gently . . . slowly move your toes and then your fingers . . . become aware of your breathing . . . inhale deeply . . . hold it . . . exhale. You feel relaxed and filled with new, quiet energy. When you are ready, open your eyes.

Golf

Stan Brown is a 31-year-old golfer with a 15 handicap, who has played since he was 12. He played in high school and college. He has stopped from time to time, once for five years. He now plays twice a week, six months out of the year. Although he often starts off well he begins looking ahead at his score, hoping he can keep it up. He then starts missing shots, trying too hard, and his game begins to fall apart. Usually after telling himself he's not playing well today, he further loses his concentration and focus, saying to himself such things as, "I can't putt today. I don't have it. I don't know what's going on, I choked on that one." He stops having fun and gets more and more serious and intense. However, a hopeful attitude endures, one which rests on making a few good shots to save face. Eventually though, he gets more uptight and worries about every shot, afraid that he will continue to blow it and look stupid to the other golfers. "I start to press and then really lose it. Pretty soon I am simply looking forward to ending the misery of my poor performance." When he plays well, he stays in the moment and has a sense of ease and confidence about his game. At those times, he wonders why he can't play that well all the time.

GOALS AND AFFIRMATIONS

We worked with Stan to make him aware of the emotions and doubts that distract him and cause him to lose confidence. He established the following goals and affirmations:

Short-Term Goals

1. To encourage and compliment myself when I play well.
2. To notice and change my negative self-talk if I'm playing poorly.
3. To start visualizing regularly, three times a week for ten minutes a day.
4. To stop blaming others or equipment or conditions when I'm playing poorly.
5. To be more relaxed and simply enjoy playing.
6. To be correctly aligned and focused for each shot.

Intermediate Goals

1. To know it is OK to make mistakes and not to worry about what others think when I blow a shot.

2. To stay in the moment, that is, don't count up my shots and look ahead.

3. To begin visualizing a shot before I make it.

4. To notice when I am tensing up and remember to breathe and allow myself to relax.

5. To acknowledge the equal importance of mental practice and physical practice.

6. To learn to execute the correct swing plane for each club.

Long-Term Goals

1. To write a mental log for each round to see where I need improvement mentally and physically.

2. To cut five strokes from my handicap this summer.

3. To review a shot visually after making it and see it perfectly executed.

4. To make it a habit to visually rehearse, hit, and review each shot in a round.

5. To make my images as specific as possible from beginning to end (seeing the ball hitting the ground, bouncing, settling on the green, disappearing in the hole, etc.)

6. To win a local tournament this summer.

Short-Term Affirmations

1. a. I encourage and support myself.
   b. I appreciate my good shots.
   c. I am confident in myself and my ability.

2. a. I tell myself positive things even when I play poorly.
   b. I notice my negative self talk and change it to positive.
   c. I am a positive person and a positive golfer.

3. a. I enjoy practicing visualizations.
   b. I visualize regularly.
   c. I visualize three times a week.
   d. I learn something valuable every time I visualize.

4. a. I am accountable for all my shots, both good and bad.
   b. I stop blaming others and my clubs for my mistakes.
   c. I am accountable and in control.

5. a. I am relaxed and playful.
   b. I enjoy playing golf just for the fun of it.
   c. Golf is fun and relaxing for me.

6. a. I am correctly aligned and focused for each shot.
   b. I have excellent form.
   c. My alignment is perfect.
   d. I have a smooth and powerful swing.

Intermediate Affirmations

1. a. It is OK to make mistakes.
   b. I let go of my mistakes and learn from them.
   c. I am free of worry about what others think of me or my performance.

2. a. I play in the moment.
   b. I am focused and centered in the moment.
   c. I play "in the now."
   d. I am free of worry about the future.

3. a. I visualize each shot before I make it.
   b. I visualize easily, consistently, and well.
   c. I visually rehearse each shot before hitting the ball.

4. a. I am relaxed.
   b. I am free of tension.
   c. It is easy for me to relax my body and mind.
   d. I breathe fully and easily.

5. a. Mental practice is important and good for me.
   b. I acknowledge the importance of mental training, rehearsal, and imagery.

6. a. I execute the correct swing planes for all clubs.
   b. My body executes the correct swing plane for all my shots.

Long-Term Affirmations

1. a. I write a mental log for each round I play.
   b. I enjoy writing a mental log for my golf game.
   c. My mental log is valuable and I learn from it.

2. a. I easily cut five strokes from my handicap this summer.
   b. I improve my game by five strokes this summer.
   c. I am shooting well and accurately.

3. a. After each shot, I review it and "see" it perfectly executed.
   b. I practice a perfect mental review after each shot.

4. a. It is my habit to rehearse, hit and review each of my shots.
   b. I enjoy rehearsing and reviewing all my shots.

5. a. I visualize very specifically and positively.
   b. I see, hear, and feel each shot perfectly.
   c. I gain perfection through visualization.

6. a. I win a local tournament this summer.
   b. I easily win a tournament.
   c. I am a winner.
   d. I am an excellent and powerful golfer.

VISUALIZATION FOR GOLF

(Begin with a progressive relaxation from chap. 4 or one that you know works for you.)

Notice how you feel as you drive into the parking lot of the club house . . . notice your sense of anticipation . . . notice that you are looking forward to practicing the things you have been working on . . . your body feels light . . . you are looking forward to using some visualization processes as you play today . . . incorporating them in an easy and gentle way.

As you approach the first tee, you can feel a sense of ease and confidence in your body . . . feel the grip of your club, your spikes in the ground and notice how good you feel to be outside . . . be aware of the smells and sounds of the life around you . . . realize how unusually relaxed and ready you feel. . . .

Imagine the course you will be playing . . . appreciate the design of the first few holes . . . where the sand traps and hazards lie . . . you might even imagine yourself having a conversation with these obstacles . . . the lake . . . the water . . . the white stakes . . . you say, "Hello there . . . I know you are out there . . . and it's O.K. I'd like to be your friend. . . . I'd also like to know if there is something I could give you besides my golf ball. . . ." The water or lake may respond. . . . "I want you to respect me. . . . I do respect you. . . . I'd like to make friends with you.... I know you are there ... and that's O.K...." You talk to the green and the out-of-bounds areas in the same way ... you make friends with the whole course by acknowledging and respecting the course ... you are free of resisting certain areas of the course ... being free of resistance, you will notice that you play at a higher level ... you relax into it and focus on your form and breathing ... your calmness and control ... as you take your practice swings, you have a sense of confidence and relaxation in your body ... you take out your tee and push it into the ground, adjusting it perfectly ... you feel your spikes gripping the ground ... you begin to visualize your club as a natural extension of your arm ... internally you have a sense of feeling solid, centered and in control ... you hit the ball with a solid impact ... hearing the sound ... it is a good, solid shot ... watch the flight of the ball as it goes down the fairway ... watch it bounce along the fairway and slowly come to rest exactly where you had envisioned it ... you are thoroughly enjoying being on the course today ... notice the weather as you hear your friends commenting on the great position of your ball ... they kid with you and compliment you on your shot ... good drive ... you move down the fairway and begin to assess the next shot you are going to make ... you assess the lie of the green, the wind and weather conditions ... you decide which club to use next ... once this is done, you let go of your intellect and allow images to come into your mind . . . just before you swing, again you see the image of hitting the ball perfectly . . . you accept this and let it go . . . relaxed and breathing you look at the ball, and swing . . . easily . . . in control . . . you feel it in your body and hear the sweet, solid sound of the ball being hit and watch the ball in the air moving along its trajectory . . . bouncing . . . rolling. . . .

After you have physically completed the shot, you mentally review the entire sequence in your mind . . . hearing the club making good, solid contact with the ball . . . you see, hear and feel the entire act of making the shot perfectly . . . with each shot, you go through this sequence of rehearsing, visualizing, feeling and reviewing again . . . you will see yourself approaching the ball, positioning your body, relaxing, taking a breath and exhaling . . . swinging and seeing the ball in flight down the fairway . . . landing in the position you desire. . . .

See yourself on each tee, swinging and hitting accurately and well . . . choosing the correct club for each shot . . . relaxing and swinging freely and well . . . hearing the sounds you want to hear . . . feeling the coordination and physical sensations of hitting the ball perfectly . . . remember that it is OK to make mistakes and that you can let go of them easily . . . you are willing to be accountable for each shot . . . you enjoy each moment of play . . . your body and shoulders are relaxed . . . you know that the mental practice of your game is as important as your physical practice . . . mental practice will improve your accuracy . . . you are calm and enjoying yourself totally. . . .

When you get to the green, see yourself assessing the green before you putt . . . the break and the roll . . . see the ball rolling perfectly along your dew line and into the hole . . . sense the speed of the ball . . . watch the ball moving toward the hole and disappearing. You might imagine a huge baseball glove popping out of the hole . . . see the ball going straight into the pocket of the glove . . . the ball naturally gravitating to the hole as if drawn in by a magnet . . . or imagine the ball having eyes and seeing where it is going . . . it sees the hole and rolls toward it perfectly on course . . . plopping in. . . .

Feel your confidence . . . remember your affirmations. . . . "I encourage and support myself. . . . I tell myself positive things when I am playing. . . . I enjoy practicing visualization. . . . I am accountable for my mistakes. . . . I am a relaxed and powerful player. . . . I enjoy golf. . . . I have excellent form and am perfectly aligned for each shot . . . . I play in the moment. . . ."

Slowly let your vision of being at the golf course slip away . . . let it go . . . begin to feel yourself in your chair or on the floor . . . notice your breathing . . . feel the relaxation in your body . . . know when you open your eyes you will be relaxed, invigorated and refreshed . . . when I count to three you will open your eyes and feel relaxed and alert . . . one . . . two . . . three. . . .

Tennis

Bob Steele is a club player. He is 35 years old and has played tennis off and on since college. He is a busy lawyer, travels often, but manages to spend an hour or so a day playing tennis. He usually spends several hours playing on the weekends. He competes in club and city tournaments. He has trouble concentrating, often getting angry during a match, whether at his doubles partner or himself. He has the tendency to cramp his forehand and sometimes hesitates before running to a shot, often arriving too late. His reaction time is fast, but his lack of mental concentration results in not being ready for a shot when he should be in position. His second serve could be faster and more accurate. His main problem is remaining focused on missed shots after they are over and dwelling on his mistakes. His concentration on past mistakes seriously interferes with his playing. He is always a much better hitter in practice than he is in a match. He blows shots, gets very angry at himself, and often loses to players who are less accomplished than himself. Though he is an expert player, these incidents have led to him doubting his ability and frustration with himself and his game.

GOALS AND AFFIRMATIONS

Short-Term Goals

1. To encourage and compliment myself after making a good shot.
2. To stop negative self-talk and focus on the moment.
3. To start supporting myself with positive statements.
4. To learn from each mistake and then to let it go.
5. To hit forehand with good form and without cramping.

Intermediate Goals

1. To encourage and support my doubles partner.
2. To control my temper and emotions while playing.
3. To let go of anger and stop dwelling on mistakes.
4. To forget a missed point and drop it mentally.
5. To focus on each shot as it comes up.
6. To play confidently and well.

Long-Term Goals

1. To play aggressively and tenaciously.
2. To have fun playing.
3. To play as well in tournaments as I do in practice.
4. To be a calm, cool, and collected player.
5. To win city mixed-doubles championship.
6. To win club championship in men's doubles.

Short-Term Affirmations

1. a. I support and encourage myself after a good shot.
   b. I appreciate my good shots.
   c. I like myself.
   d. I tell myself 'good job' after a good point.
2. a. I use positive self talk often.
   b. I am a positive person.
   c. I turn negative experiences into positive ones.
   d. I learn from my mistakes.
3. a. I support myself with positive statements.
   b. I am a confident player.
   c. I believe in myself and my abilities.
   d. I am an excellent tennis player.
4. a. I play each shot in the moment.
   b. I am focused in the moment.

c. I focus totally on each shot as it comes to me.
d. I am focused in the here and now.

5. a. I have an excellent forehand.
b. I hit a forehand with perfect form and balance.
c. I feel the forehand shot perfectly and am ready.
d. I see the forehand shot perfectly.

Intermediate Affirmations

1. a. I encourage and support my doubles partner.
b. I like and respect my doubles partner.
c. I enjoy playing with my doubles partner.

2. a. I am in control of my temper on and off the court.
b. I am free of anger and resentment.
c. I am a relaxed and confident player.

3. a. I let go of my anger.
b. I let go of past mistakes and move forward.
c. I forgive myself easily when I make a mistake.
d. I am free of anger.

4. a. I let go of a missed shot.
b. It is OK to let go of my mistakes.
c. I learn from my mistakes and it helps my game.

5. a. I am focused and in control.
   b. I have excellent concentration.
   c. I focus on each shot as it comes up.
   d. I am alert and ready at all times in a match.

6. a. I am a confident player.
   b. I play well and with control.
   c. I am an excellent tennis player.

Long-Term Affirmations

1. a. I am an aggressive player and keep my control.
   b. I am a tenacious player.

2. a. I enjoy playing tennis.
   b. Playing tennis is fun and good for me.
   c. I play for the enjoyment of the sport and love of the game.
   d. I enjoy winning and doing well.

3. a. I play as well in tournaments as I do when practicing.
   b. I love playing in tournaments.
   c. I am an excellent tournament player.

4. a. I am a calm, cool, and collected player.
   b. I am calm and confident.

5. a. We win the city mixed-doubles championships.
   b. We win mixed-doubles tournaments often.
   c. We are an excellent mixed doubles team.

6. a. We win the club championship in men's doubles.
   b. We are excellent doubles players and enjoy playing together.
   c. We play well together and win often.

VISUALIZATION FOR TENNIS

(Begin with a progressive relaxation technique from chap. 4 before starting this visualization.)

Imagine yourself as you arrive at the tennis courts . . . see people playing . . . feel the air, the environment . . . hear the sounds of balls and racquets . . . feel the sun on your back . . . enjoy anticipating the match . . . experience the feeling in your stomach and in your body . . . you are a little nervous but very ready . . . remembering that these are common feelings before you play a match. . . .

You begin to hit on the court . . . hitting with long, powerful strokes . . . hitting smoothly . . . rapidly . . . accurately . . . feeling relaxed and confident . . . remember some of your affirmations as you are warming up. . . . "I encourage myself after a good shot. . . . I am a positive person. . . . I turn negative experiences into positive ones. . . . I support myself. . . . I am a confident player. . . . I believe in myself and my abilities. . . . I play each shot in the moment and I am very focused as I play. . . . I am in control of my temper and am free of anger and resentment. . . . I am confident, relaxed, and play with good form. . . ."

The match has started . . . you are moving well . . . you are light and quick . . . you are focused . . . as the ball comes to you on each shot, you concentrate perfectly on the ball . . . you establish a rhythm of bounce, hit, bounce, hit . . . hitting with power, strength, and accuracy . . . as you hit each ball, you see it going over the net exactly where you want it to go . . . you feel the perfection in your body as you hit the shot . . . you hear the sound of the ball hitting your racquet in the right spot . . . notice yourself enjoying the match immensely . . . you are glad to be out on this beautiful day playing . . . and playing well . . . you feel relaxed . . . loose . . . you are breathing out as you hit each ball . . . your forehand is light . . . floating . . . accurate . . . you feel light and you are ready for each shot when it comes to you . . . you easily place the shot wherever you want it to go . . . with accuracy and ease. . . .

See yourself getting into position . . . the ball coming to your forehand, you are in the perfect position to hit it . . . you hit it and watch it go straight to the place on the court where you want it to go . . . you hit a forehand crosscourt, placing it well . . . the ball returns . . . you hit a backhand crosscourt . . . a forehand straight down the line . . . deep in the corner . . . a serve comes to your backhand, you stroke perfectly, hitting it down the line . . . another winner . . . another serve to you, coming to your forehand, you put a nice drop shot just over the net . . . your opponent scrambles to get it and hits a high lob . . . you settle into position and quickly execute an overhead smash . . . you receive another serve . . . to your backhand and execute a deep backhand crosscourt shot, you feel powerful and controlled . . . experience your body sensations . . . determination, relaxation, control, quickness . . . knowing that you are right on . . . continue to see the ball coming to you . . . you hit each stroke with power, accuracy, and control . . . if you miss a shot, you notice what you did in error, make the necessary adjustments, and let it go . . . coming back to the present moment for the next point . . . all that exists is one shot at a time . . . one point at a time . . . you are living and playing in the moment . . . moment to moment . . . experience your body enjoying the sensations of play and competition . . . enjoying the aggressiveness . . . playing well . . . centered and focused . . . point by point . . . being alert and ready at the line . . . rushing the net with confidence . . . experiencing the feeling of confidence in your body and mind . . . telling yourself that you are an excellent player. . . .

Experience the power you feel as a good and competent player . . . a player who wins . . . a player who gives everything and plays the best he knows how . . . you have achieved your goals . . . you have played well and feel proud and complete . . . allow yourself to have it all as you slowly let go of the image . . . let it float away and leave your mind . . . come slowly back to your physical space . . . reconnect with your breathing and the feel of the chair or floor beneath you . . . move your toes and then your fingers . . . breathe . . . when I count to three you may open your eyes . . . one . . . two . . . three. . . .

I AM BALANCED AND IN CONTROL

CHAPTER TWELVE

The Use of Videotapes in Coaching

The room is dim and you sit quietly with your athletes watching their last competition on the screen before you. You see the mistakes: someone missed a cue, someone lost his or her concentration. You point it out. You want them to learn. There . . . just a minute; rewind . . . there, they did it right. This you also point out so they will know. Doing it right is important. The video continues and as a coach you scrutinize, analyze, and teach. Your hope is that the athletes will learn and make changes. Their next competition will be better.

Videotape has been a significant coaching tool for several years. As it becomes refined, financially more accessible, and easier to use, this piece of training "equipment" will be universally used. But even now it is mobile, relatively inexpensive, and generally effective in helping a coach demonstrate an athlete's or team's form, function, and mistakes.

Videotaping competitive performance can be effective, enlightening, and exceedingly valuable. It can also harm an athlete's or team's mental self-concept.

More and more coaches and athletes will take advantage of videotapes' present uses, which we will describe. And we will look beyond this to the potential or only partially explored ways in which videotapes can be used to improve athletic performance.

Present Uses in Coaching

We interviewed three coaches about their use of videotapes in coaching.

Paul Brothers, Marist High School girl's basketball coach, uses videotapes in three ways: 1) filming each individual player performing free throws and jump shots, dribbling, and rebounding, 2) filming each home game, and 3) viewing training films.

The filming of individual players is done a couple of times a year, mainly before the season begins. Videos are shot during practice. Each girl watches the tapes, knowing how it felt to do the move. "It is instant feedback and the biggest impact is made because it is fresh. The biggest problem in girl's basketball is teaching them how to jump. We need a good technique tape that is geared to women. Most basketball tapes are not high quality and the content isn't very good. Videotaping is very useful but it takes a lot of time. We have to share the gym. We'd use it more if we had the time and space to do it. Mainly, when we film the games, we look for the positive. We show them where they're supposed to be and we try to pick up technique. After the season starts, we just don't have the time to work on technique much."

Ed Boyd, the women's gymnastics coach at the University of Oregon, also uses videotapes extensively in the pre-season. "Most commercial videos are too basic. They are really not for the competitive gymnasts. We use a lot of pre-recorded tapes of the top gymnasts in World Championships. We see a trick we like, we break it down into all its separate parts, and then we tape our athletes performing the move to see where they are in terms of technique."

During the pre-season (mid-September through December), the gymnastics team uses the videotape at least three times a week, sometimes every day. In a typical workout the athletes start on the vault to get warmed up, do new elements, and then each athlete is taped for the same move. Four or five shots are taken of each person. Then the gymnasts go back and work on the technique. For instance, in teaching a double back on the floor, the coaches videotape the timers, put the young woman in an overhead spotting device, and have her go through the trick, eventually doing it with only a hand spot and then with no spot at all. This entire process is videotaped so she can see her progress and form as she learns the trick. It takes two to six months to learn, depending on the athlete.

"Also during the pre-season, we choreograph the dances when the gymnasts are just learning a routine. The next day they can flip it on to see the sequence of what to do next. It helps them mentally memorize their routines quickly. The hardest event is the beam. It is the most mental of all. It needs utmost concentration. We watch and concentrate on the techniques as much as possible. We give them lots of mental practice. The image they see on the tapes is visualized later in their own minds. We teach them to see, hear, smell, and feel the event in as much detail as possible. The videotapes help the athlete to mentally visualize her moves before she executes them."

An important caution here. When using videotapes of your athletes either in workouts or in competition, keep their viewing and analysis of mistakes to a minimum. If an athlete consistently sees herself performing incorrectly, it further cements that image in her subconscious and makes her more prone to continue committing the same mistake. This prolongs the time it takes to correct the problem. Because watching videotapes is such a powerful learning tool, the athlete should consistently see the correct and perfect way a certain movement should be performed.

While interviewing Coach Boyd, he told a story that shows the power of the visual process.

"In 1980, I began learning about visualization. I was up at summer camp teaching. I wanted to teach this young girl a tsukara vault. She was a strong vaulter with good vaulting ability, but she had never done this trick before. We did a lot of the lead-up, which is a half turn on the horse, where you have your hands on the horse. Each day after we did this, we would go through a relaxation process and then concentrate on the trick and the muscles that were used for the trick. She would tighten the muscles we figured she should be tightening for the sequence. We did it a lot slower than it happens. We did this every day for about two weeks. Then we pulled up a large crash pad and she was able to do the trick without even a spot from the very first time she did the movement. It was exciting and scary all at the same time. It was like, 'Wow, look what I did!' and then, 'What did I do?!' Both ends hit me at once. I had been to a couple of different gymnastics clinics where people were just starting to play with visualization. This was before it had become a real big thing. I haven't done much since then because I didn't feel that I was qualified to do the mental thing. I am qualified as a coach, but in this particular case, I went a little beyond. It is hard to find someone who will be so receptive. I think she was probably a one in a million chance. I could probably do that with other people and not have it happen that way again. She was so receptive to it, it was amazing. When we went through the relaxation, I think that she really went under. She wasn't really conscious of anything going on around her. I think she was totally able to immerse herself in it."

Mike Manley, former Olympic steeplechase champion and coach, uses the videotape extensively in his coaching and training of elite runners. Manley uses the videotape in four basic ways: 1) for injury prevention, 2) to develop efficiency in biomechanics, 3) for strategy options in racing, 4) for conditioning or technique.

Manley tapes his athletes on the track, and then they view the tapes together while he critiques their form and style. To prevent injury, the athlete is taped running on a treadmill so that foot plant and style can be studied. Manley looks for pronation, supination, and other irregularities. The athlete is photographed from the front, rear, and sides for a comparison. If the foot strike has certain problems, the athlete can consider doing strengthening exercises to help the problem or wearing different shoes. The videotape can also be shared with the sports medicine physician for diagnosis and treatment.

"We use videotape to get the athlete to see what he/she is doing. He/she can visualize where the weak points are. When you can point things out and see yourself, it is much easier to make changes in style. The point is to have the runner run as relaxed as possible with rhythm and fluidity, conserving energy as much as possible. Someone's body type may not permit them to run with the perfect form and grace of athletes like Mary Decker or Sebastian Coe. We emphasize good economical form, concentrating on foot strike, push off, knee lift, hip tilt, posture, relaxed shoulders, rhythmic arm swing, head up with no bouncing, and no clinching of fists. To run efficiently, the runner must keep in mind the proper techniques."

Ideally, two or three good runners should be taped as examples of good style and form. Then the coach could tape the subject on the last part of the tape for comparison. The tape would be half instructional and half personal so the athlete can see the comparison quickly and easily. Also helpful would be a tape of a variety of circuit training exercises for runners to show them the proper form and sequence of the training. In technical events such as sprinting, the more visual feedback the better. In long-distance running, it is not as necessary except for achieving focus and concentration. Twice a week is about right for filming technique. For the long distances, Manley films every two months or so. It takes time for change to occur. Sometimes the change is very minute. The athlete is learning to monitor how his or her body feels as well as how it looks. Manley maintains that to run faster an athlete must concentrate on efficiency of form, relaxation, rhythm, and fluidity. If he or she has all these things, the athlete will be more energy efficient.

"With our best runners, we only tape them once or twice a year. The tape is better used in terms of strategy. I'll videotape a race and we'll sit around and discuss the strategy afterward. With steeplechase, we work on technique early in the season, maybe twice every three weeks or so. After the season starts, we work on strategy.

"One way videotape could be used would be to photograph the race with a pace clock and analyze the splits to see where the athlete slowed down. What he/she was doing and why. You run differently on the track performing for the camera than you do in a race. It's important to film both. Catching a runner at the end of a race would be important in terms of form and whether his/her form fell apart at the end. Those are the things you look for.

"In learning to use the camera, you just have to practice with it a lot. I took several wrong angles, too close, too far away, etc. It helps to set it all up in advance and to have someone to help you. Train someone else to do it the way you want it done so you can be with the athletes. If you're trying to coach and run the camera at the same time, neither is going to be the quality you want. A tripod helps the stability and I'd advise using one."

In the Future

It seems only common sense to see a tremendous expansion of the use of videotapes in the future. Its uses are unlimited. A few coaches are, at present, peeking their lenses over the horizon. A small number of athletes have found they benefit from using a sensory deprivation tank, or float tank, as part of their standard training process. Some float tanks are equipped with small videoscreens in the lid that closes overhead. While floating in a state of total physical and mental relaxation in complete darkness, you watch videotapes of yourself going through your event perfectly or technique tapes of a master athlete in their event. Because the floating athlete is in such a deep state of relaxation, the pictures he or she sees of each movement done to perfection are deeply imprinted on the cells of the brain. Mentally, you have an absolutely clear vision of how you should physically perform. When you find yourself in your next competition or workout, you perform more effectively. This can be considered a form of guided visualization, one step in comprehensive mental training. The whole process of videotape viewing can be considered simply one form of visualization.

In the future, "video-visualization" may move into the world of dreams. Suppose an athlete dreams of performing significantly above his or her present level. A script of this dream could be developed, along with cartoon footage representing the athlete and the dreamed of event. The athlete or team, with the assistance of the coach, would be responsible for the content of the script, guaranteeing the perfection of the language and the movements pictured. A videotape would then be made and shown over and over again to the athlete as a visualization tool. Research now shows that this athlete can accomplish his or her dream much sooner than thought possible and at a higher level than believed. "Pre-programming" can lead to subconscious physical building and preparation for an actual physical performance that is not presently physically possible.

Here is another possibility. You, as a coach, have an injured athlete. A video program on that specific injury, its physical appearance, cause, and the healing process could be produced to help the athlete understand the why and what of the injury and when he or she can begin to train again. One step beyond this would be a video, again in cartoon form, of the healing of the actual injury. The athlete would see the tendons, bones, or muscles knitting, healing, and becoming well and whole, imprinting in his or her mind the image of the injury mending and becoming strong and well. This, in turn, would signal to the body the correct way to heal and support this process. Above all, it centers the athlete's focus on healing rather than on frustration over not training or a "weakness" of the body.

These are simply a few of the possible future uses of videotapes in the athletic field. The use of videotapes in coaching is still very much in its infancy. The options are almost limitless. The use of video-visualization is continually proven to be an effective and powerful tool in the training and achieving of an athlete's highest performance potential.

(Parts of this chapter appeared in an article in the coaches' section of *Women's Sports & Fitness* May, 1985.)

CHAPTER THIRTEEN

Mental Training for a Team

This chapter shows how we work with a team. In this case, it was the University of Oregon women's tennis team.

In the years between age 10 and 22, I played tennis. I always saw myself as a rather mediocre player, although in looking back on it, I was better than I thought at the time. I won a few tournaments in doubles, and was number three on the teams in high school and college in El Paso where I grew up. I took numerous lessons from Margaret Varner, our local celebrity. While I never quite mastered my tennis game, I mastered the negative game totally, doing everything that I have spent the last few years teaching people not to do. I choked, blew my concentration, cursed myself, mentally abused myself, and considered myself a total loser when it came to tennis. The more my coach told me to "relax!" the more I tensed. I was a master of self-defeat. Had I only known then what I know now! I am well aware of what goes on in the mind of the average player. I once had every mental affliction known to man (and woman) on the court.

Dr. Kay Porter

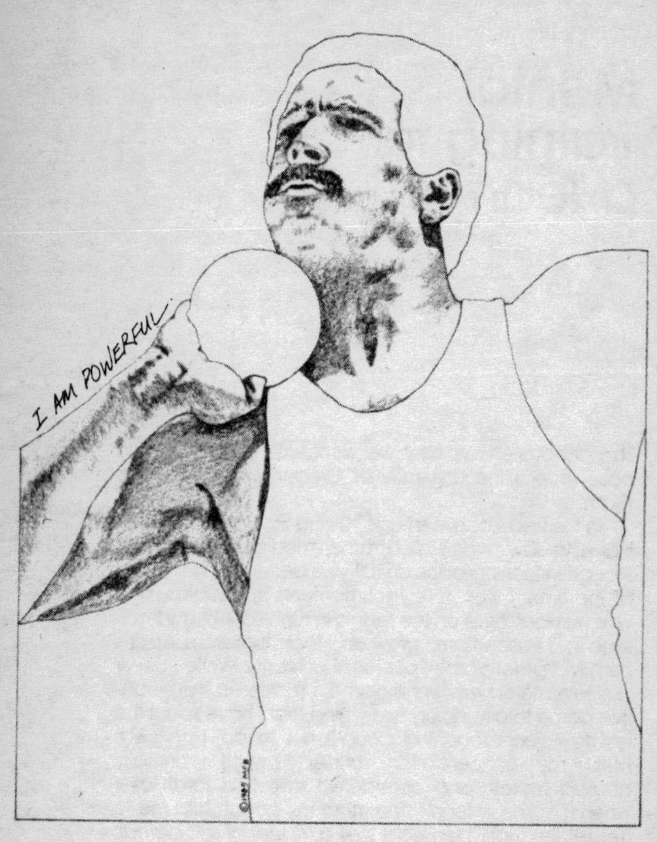
I AM POWERFUL

It was with this questionable background that we approached our work with the University of Oregon women's tennis team.

Nancy Osborne, the coach, knew of our work with runners and other university athletes and asked us if we could work with her team. We readily agreed and began our program in late fall 1983. We met with the team over a period of six months, every four to six weeks. Actually, if we were recommending a team time schedule, we would suggest meeting every two to three weeks. Nancy, however, was quite skilled in leading closed-eye visualizations and relaxation sessions, so she did much of the week to week follow-up. All of us had fun working together. The team learned a lot, and so did we—such as making sure that most visualization practice done by the player was done during her progressive relaxation session and not while on the court. To our surprise, the players were trying to visualize their next shot as the ball was approaching, rather than focusing "in the moment." Although some players may do this successfully, especially in sports such as basketball, to others it can be quite confusing and may lead to a poorer performance.

The Training

When working with any team, we begin with an hour presentation outlining the highlights of our program "Mental Training for Peak Athletic Performance." As you know, the main topics are physical relaxation, goal setting, positive self-statements (affirmations), concentration and focusing, guided visualizations of the event or match, self-nurturing, and keeping a mental training log.

After discussing the details of our philosophy, which is "what you 'see' is what you get," we begin with goal setting. The homework assignment is to write out the team's and individual athlete's short-term, intermediate, and long-term goals for the next year. The team writes the affirmations for the team goals. In the following sessions, we teach them relaxation skills and lead them in various guided visualizations of old competitions, new competitions, and other content areas. Much of the time is spent discussing what to do mentally for certain problem areas in competition. They are taught to center, a physical technique discussed in chapter 4. They are taught to "calm down" and to "psych up" themselves. Often, we will work with a player or athlete individually, doing an in-depth interview and analyzing every aspect of his or her game and what he or she does in terms of mental self-talk. Players are urged to keep a mental training log of every match so the mental dynamics of their playing can be tracked and analyzed.

We stress the importance of self-responsibility and self-accountability and the importance of taking responsibility for one's own reaction to what happens in life and in competition—that is, not blaming others. We advocate making anger and disappointment productive rather than letting them lead to depression. We emphasize talking to oneself positively and practicing mental rehearsal and imagery—seeing, feeling, and hearing an entire match or game for oneself, and mentally experiencing each team member in the correct position, performing perfectly. Players are easily able to do this after practicing mental rehearsal in class under our guidance. We have also made tapes for individuals that enable them to follow a guided visualization of our making, like those contained in some of our chapters and in the appendix. Some prefer this method to creating their own scenarios.

The underlying philosophy of what we discuss with teams and individual athletes is that we and we alone create our own reality with our mind. We are constantly making choices that dictate our performance level, our reality of the game, and, when dealing with a team, the overall performance and outcome for that team. Any athlete, and especially one on a team, must learn to be accountable for his or her choices. If each member does his or her part without blaming others, the team will stay in balance and will succeed. A major problem for many teams is the problem of blame and resentment. This upsets team harmony and limits performance.

Psychology of a Good Team Competitor

In interviewing Nancy, the tennis coach, herself a fine tennis player, we asked what she thought was the psychological makeup of a good team competitor. She discussed the following points: (1) A good competitor has to have the ability to concentrate, to focus her attention for a long period of time on the task and to maintain that focus—perhaps through meditation, learning the skills of focusing. The calming effect is fine and would help the player concentrate on the task at hand. (2) Someone like Chris Evert-Lloyd—she never gives up. She is assertive and hustles for every shot—without monopolizing the court if she is playing doubles but assisting when needed. (3) A top competitor must have discipline—again, the ability to concentrate, the willingness to work, to sacrifice. Sort of a "doingness" and, combined with that, an ability to relax and focus on the moment, centering themselves, resulting in a "beingness." A combination of the two creates a balanced player and helps to balance the team. A good competitor has the willingness to do all the things physically that a great athlete has to do, combined with a psychological demeanor that shows in the body through confidence, competence, and accountability. The athlete also talks "nicely" to herself as well as to other members of the team, never saying negative things aloud or in self-talk. (4) Last, the player takes the time to totally relax and to nurture herself in a kind way to be of greater benefit to herself and to the team. Learning this balance of beingness and doingness is essential for championship playing and in preventing burnout. The good competitor brings positive energy to the team from which all members can draw when needed.

Mind Talk

Much time in our sessions is devoted to discussing what to do mentally when dealing with mind-talk and mind-chatter. As we described in chapter 3, our recommendations concerning mind-chatter are twofold: (1) Whenever players start to get down on themselves mentally, we encourage them to notice it and say something like, "OK, you're doing it again, come on, let's change this," and begin with simple affirmations such as: "I am centered;" "I am focused;" "I am in control." Other statements will help: "OK, calm down. You know what to do; feel your power in your center (or solar plexus, etc.)." Or "You know you can play well; relax and concentrate on each point." And then, we get them to let go, to move their focus back to the game and their responsibilities. (2) When players are upset with their playing, we ask them to be especially nice to themselves in their self-talk and not to use phrases such as, "That was stupid; you're stupid." Or "You're really messing this up." Statements such as the following are much more beneficial: "Come on, you're OK; you know you are a good player; calm down, it's OK." This is also an excellent time to say one's affirmations and refocus on form or breathing. Saying one's "word" from the visualization in chapter 5 can be very helpful and calming at these times.

In dealing with the University of Oregon tennis team, a major concern was what they did with their minds between points or between games. Since the time between points is short, the player can practice being more focused on the coming point—saying affirmations when walking back to position or thinking of short strategies to stop the opponent. When returning to the baseline, it is important to give one's full attention to either the serve or the return, focusing entirely "in the moment" rather than thinking about a lost point or thinking ahead in the game or match. In between games, the player has more time to figure out strategy and how to implement that strategy. Simple psyching "games" include assertiveness in body language, questioning bad calls rather than stewing about them silently, maintaining eye contact with an opponent, carrying the body with confidence and control, and calling shots decisively. These are not examples of bad sportsmanship, they are merely ways of maintaining psychological control of oneself and the match.

Mental Log Keeping for a Team

Among elite athletes, the strategy of analyzing the match or competition is valuable for what they learn of their own playing and that of their opponent. The mental side of the match or game is crucial, in that one sees and acknowledges one's negative self-talk and how it hurts one's playing. It is also important to acknowledge positive self-talk and how it helped one's game. For a written comprehensive mental training log of competitions (entry written within twenty-four hours of the competition), team members write all positive and negative thoughts and energy they can remember during the match or game and how these thoughts or energy did or did not help them play their best. Many times, if two or three players on a team perform poorly or make mistakes that cost the team points, the energy level of the team as a whole will fall. The more the energy depresses each member's spirits, the poorer the team as a whole will do. If this is a familiar experience, it is important for the team as a whole to write down what the negative thoughts and feelings were and what it did to the energy and performance of the team. They should then discuss this with one another and the coach and let it go, learning from the experience and moving on.

The team's keeping a mental log also serves as a catharsis (purging) of the match or game. The player and team, after having written in the log and discussed the matter together, are free to drop the emotions and intensity of the match or game and focus on the future. This process leads to maximum learning, and the players can see the dynamics of what happens for them mentally on the court or in the game. Telling yourself that, "I did the best I could at the time" is true; it may or may not be of any consolation. The only consolation may be in knowing that you are working on the mental factors that have defeated you in the past and that you are making progress for future competitions.

Guided Visualizations

At the end of every session, we conduct a "closed-eye process" or "guided visualization." In these guided visualizations, we start with progressive relaxation and follow it with a visualization that takes the athletes through the whole match or game, beginning with their warm-up and following the entire match or game to its conclusion. Though an athlete's focus should be primarily on himself or herself, it is also very important to experience all other team members playing perfectly and helping one another. In one session we had the Oregon team imagine their best match: who, what, where, and when. We had them see, hear, and feel the environment, the opponent, the weather, and all conditions as fully as possible. They imagined their feelings and thoughts, how they felt physically and mentally as they played, all their feelings of control and competence, and doing it all perfectly. We had them "see" themselves playing with smoothness and control and feeling themselves to be psychologically superior.

Visualizations such as these can be given to teams as a group or on a cassette tape, so the players can easily reproduce the situation. Once players learn the process, they can do the visualization without supervision.

How Did the Team Do?

The feedback we received from the team was interesting. We had not anticipated they would try to use extensive visualization while playing a match. This interfered with their playing. Recommending that they simply focus on short affirmations or short visual images during a match solved the problem. The team felt the relaxation helped them most and that it was best practiced before bed. The hardest part for them was controlling their emotions and learning to let go of a bad shot or shots without dwelling on the missed points. This also is a matter of consistent practice. What helped most during matches was calming their minds and not thinking at all except for short phrases or words such as: "calm," "relax," or "you're OK!"

As a team, they were more successful as the season went on. One of their biggest goals was to do well against their rival, the University of Washington, at the end of the year. Although they did not succeed in beating Washington, they won more matches than they ever had previously. They were pleased and happy that they achieved their goal. Players who practiced these techniques were enthusiastic about continuing mental training the next year.

Any of these techniques can be applied to amateurs as well as male and female club players, regardless of age. As with physical practice, mental training can achieve worthwhile results if the players and team are committed and are willing to practice the techniques weekly or daily. The processes are simple and can be easily mastered. Having done the mental preparation, a team can always say, "We have the psychological edge over our opponent."

APPENDIX A

General Affirmations

AFFIRMATIONS FOR ATHLETIC PERFORMANCE

- I am a strong and fluid athlete.
- I am as good as any other athlete at the competition today.
- I am relaxed and ready to go.
- My body is healthy and well trained.
- I am confident and ready.
- I listen to my body and it serves me well.
- I love my body.
- I am powerful and balanced.
- I am in control and focused.
- I am the greatest.
- I am a well trained and competent athlete.
- I am performing pain free.
- I am reaching my goals and realizing my peak.
- I enjoy training and competing.
- I enjoy being athletic and caring for my body.
- I trust my body and its strength.
- I am successful and winning.

AFFIRMATIONS FOR WEIGHT CONTROL

- I like my body.
- I eat only healthy foods.
- My clothes fit me well and are comfortable.
- I am healthy and fit.
- I enjoy a sugar-free diet.
- I like taking care of my body.
- I am maintaining good eating habits.
- I enjoy eating a low fat and low sugar diet.
- I am losing weight every week.
- My body is healthy and happy.
- I am thin and fit.
- I am in control of my weight.
- I enjoy looking trim and healthy.
- I like myself and the way I look.
- I have a healthy and slender body.
- I enjoy physical exercise.
- I am satisfied with healthy food.

AFFIRMATIONS FOR HEALTH AND HEALING

- I am caring for my body and my health.
- I am free of illness.
- I remain fit and strong while healing.
- I am healing well and quickly.
- I appreciate my body and my health.
- I am healthy in mind and body.
- My fitness remains at a high level even while I am injured and healing.

- My body regenerates quickly.
- My body heals quickly and well.
- My __________ (injured part) heals quickly and well. I am well and healthy. My body heals itself. My body is rested and rejuvenated.

AFFIRMATIONS FOR LIFE

- I am a beautiful and healthy person.
- I am prosperous and happy.
- I am in control of my life.
- I am loved and loving.
- I am relaxed and in control.
- I enjoy nourishing myself and those around me.
- I enjoy letting others give to me.
- I am playful and open-hearted.
- I trust myself and others.
- I am capable and competent.
- I am responsible for what I experience.
- I am changing all negative thoughts.
- I am free of fear.
- I have abundance in my life.
- I am intelligent and competent.
- I am a gentle and complete man.
- I am a beautiful, powerful woman, sharing my heart with you.
- I enjoy taking time for myself and my needs.
- I am flexible.
- I enjoy giving and receiving.
- I am important and I count.
- I am forgiving and gentle.

- I believe in myself.
- I am calm and peaceful, giving myself permission to relax.
- I am creating my own reality exactly the way I want it.

APPENDIX B

Guided Visualizations

GUIDED VISUALIZATION FOR A 10K ROAD RACE

(Use the progressive relaxation in chap. 4. before starting this visualization.)

Begin to see yourself arriving at the race area. See the starting line. It is a 10K race on the road. Notice the crowds of people and hear them talking among themselves. . . . seeing and hearing all the sights and sounds of a festive 10K race . . . the colorful T-shirts, the fun runners, the serious competitors . . . feel the nervousness in your gut . . . that old familiar feeling and know that it is your normal pre-occupation with a race . . . remembering that the minute you start, all the feelings of nervousness disappear . . . it is all part of the pre-race psyching you do for yourself while standing in the line for your last pit stop. . . .

As you start your warm-up routine . . . your stretching . . . whatever routine you do to warm up, take pleasure in those special moments in your life . . . all the times you reached your goal and did your best . . . see yourself doing your strides . . . the strong, powerful movements of your legs stretching out . . . your body feels good . . . it feels strong. Both your mind and body are anticipating this race . . . you are looking forward to it. Even though you get nervous, you know how good it feels to run hard and how good you feel at the end . . . that sense of euphoria and feeling of accomplishment . . . you know that it is always worth it . . . the nervousness is just part of the game and part of the way you play . . . you acknowledge it and let it go . . . let it slide away. . . .

See yourself in your favorite running clothes, taking off your warm-ups . . . getting ready to start the race . . . you are completely focused within and you are taking your last few strides . . . stretching out . . . feeling your muscles warm and supple in your body. Take your place at the starting line . . . hear the instructions from the starter . . . hear the sound of the gun. . . .

You take off . . . you are familiar with the course . . . you have seen the course before . . . feel all the people around you . . . bumping, breathing, some still talking . . . you know some of them . . . you have your eye out for certain runners . . . you know who they are . . . you know what your strategy is . . . feel your body moving easily . . . your body is like something which has been cooped up in a cage and is now being let free . . . your body is free to run. . . .

The first mile always feels so good . . . the adrenalin is pumping . . . you have been looking forward to this race . . . you have trained hard and you are in good physical shape . . . you are ready. See yourself on the course . . .

focusing on your form, your body, your competitors . . . you are in perfect rhythm and synch with your environment . . . feel the sun or the wind or perhaps a little rain on your body . . . the physical sensations of the weather on your face . . . feel your body working, holding its form, running strong . . . say a few of your affirmations to yourself. . . . "I feel good; I am running very well and within myself. . . ."

When you reach the first-mile mark and hear the time, what is it? Are you on pace? Are you a little fast? What are you telling yourself? . . . Imagine yourself running the goal pace you have set . . . feeling comfortable . . . you can feel the pavement under your feet, the wind in your face . . . your body is warmed up now and feels good. Listen to the sound of your shoes striking the ground and the footfalls of runners around you . . . you are maintaining a very comfortable pace . . . you focus on your form and your breathing . . . steady, rhythmic . . . feeling in complete control of yourself . . . notice where you are on the course . . . see yourself running powerfully and in control. . . .

You reach the two-mile mark . . . you check your time . . . right on schedule . . . your pace is good and you keep it up, faintly noticing familiar parts of the course going by . . . you know where you are . . . the three mile mark is coming up soon. You pass it, hearing your time again . . . check your pace and how you are doing . . . do you need to pick it up? You know that when you change the pace, you feel better . . . it gives you a renewed burst of energy . . . as fartlek always does . . . you surge . . . and stabilize

. . . surge and . . . stabilize . . . you notice that the four-mile mark is just ahead . . . that was quick . . . thank your body for the fine job it is doing . . . your body is in good shape and it serves you well. . . .

Four miles is where the race begins for you . . . it is where you start using your strategy. See yourself passing the four-mile mark . . . hear your time read . . . you make your adjustments accordingly. If you are off your pace and slow, you start to pick it up . . . you know your body is ready . . . if there is pain from exertion, you welcome that pain like an old friend . . . it is all part of the race . . . if you start any negative self-talk, you merely acknowledge it and gently let it go, coming back to your form and affirmations . . . you pick up the pace . . . if you feel a little tiredness in your body, acknowledge it and turn your concentration to your breathing . . . you know you may feel like this when you push hard and reach for your goals . . . you know that you are strong and well conditioned and you have been training very well . . . you know your body will come through for you . . . bring your focus back to your breathing and your form. . . .

Imagine energy breathed in and tiredness breathed out . . . on the inhale, feel the energy coming into your body . . . on the exhale, feel the tiredness leaving your body. All that new oxygen is going to your muscles to provide them with strength and new energy. . . . "I am strong; I am running well; I am running in complete control and within myself; my body is well conditioned; I feel good. . . ." . . . think of your affirmations and say them to yourself in rhythm with your pace and form . . .

your shoulders are relaxed . . . your body is centered . . . your legs are lifting with your knees high . . . your form is good. . . .

Some runners are moving up on you . . . as they begin to pass, you pick it up and stay with them . . . you don't let them get by . . . you know they will eventually tire . . . you know you are playing a waiting game . . . a psyching game . . . you know that you are just as strong as they are . . . when they least expect it, you pull ahead . . . you surge for maybe sixty yards . . . not looking back . . . just surging ahead . . . you know that you can leave them far behind . . . you have broken their concentration and focus . . . they will not pass you again. You feel the renewal of energy and exhilaration. . . .

You see another runner ahead of you . . . you quietly move up . . . then put on another surge . . . passing him so quickly he is taken by surprise . . . you know that you will stay ahead of him also. After the surging, you feel your body relax again . . . you hear the five mile time . . . another quick mile . . . your time is good and you know that there is only a little over a mile to go. . . .

You feel the excitement in your body . . . another rush of adrenalin . . . this is it . . . you know you can do it. Concentrate on your form . . . pick up the pace again . . . notice your breathing . . . relax your shoulders . . . another runner ahead . . . you surge again . . . maintaining a strong pace . . . passing and going ahead . . . you continue passing people during this last mile as you increase your pace . . . the mile passes quickly as you pick off people. Suddenly you see the six-mile mark ahead, realize there are only a couple of minutes left, and begin your kick . . . you see the finish line . . . you begin to hear the crowd . . . surging, kicking . . . in perfect control . . . you see the last opponent in front of you . . . you surge again . . . just as you pass him, you cross the finish line . . . you have succeeded . . . you hear your time . . . you know you have achieved your goal. . . .

You feel euphoric, happy, tired and content . . . you have done your best . . . hands on your hips . . . gasping for breath . . . breathing hard, you tell yourself. . . . "I did it! . . . thank you legs, lungs, arms . . . thank you . . . thank you mind." You walk . . . start jogging for your warm-down . . . feeling happy knowing that you have run your best . . . a feeling of accomplishment and completion . . . all the mental and physical training you have done has culminated in this moment . . . knowing you have done your best . . . thanking yourself and your body . . . knowing that you can do it again, both physically and mentally, any time you wish. . . . Become aware of your body now, sitting in the chair or lying on the floor. Feel the contentment as you let go of the picture and slowly come back to your relaxed breathing and the peace and stillness. Breathe in . . . hold in . . . exhale. Say your affirmations and think of your goal . . . breathe . . . exhale . . . breathe . . . exhale . . . be aware of your body and your breathing . . . feel your chest rise and fall with each breath . . . move your fingers and then your toes . . . you are relaxed yet full of new energy . . . when you are ready, open your eyes and reconnect with your present space. Thank your body for its strength and power, its speed and its health . . . give yourself permission to rest, knowing that anytime you aim at a goal, you can feel it, see it or hear it in your mind's eye and eventually have it in reality.

GUIDED VISUALIZATION FOR A MARATHON

(Use the progressive relaxation technique in chap. 4.)

It is the beginning of a marathon. There are balloons and banners, colors and noise. You are standing in a crowd of runners. You can hear them talking to one another, and you can smell their presence and excitement. Some people are yelling, smiling, or talking, and some are silent. You stretch, feeling the tightness, the readiness in your muscles. It is a cloudy day, cool with a slight breeze that moves your hair and makes a noise in the trees by the side of the road. You feel the excitement in your stomach. You take several deep breaths and look down at your feet. It is quiet for a moment . . . the gun goes off . . . and everyone starts moving.

Slowly your feet begin feeling the hardness of the pavement, someone bumps you as they pass by. Be aware of your feelings as two or three more runners pass you, finding their own pace. You know you have 26 miles to go and you are aware of your goal. Notice how your body feels and what your words are to yourself as you pass the one-mile mark and hear your time. Are you on schedule? Have you gone out too fast? You feel the wind against your chest as you find your rhythm and begin to move out of the crowd. Is it cooling or is it pushing at you, slowing you down? You pass someone and then another as you reach six miles. Be aware of your breathing. Are you sweating yet? How do your legs feel? Just notice and then let go of the thoughts. Come back to your breathing as you continue along the road as it turns and becomes rougher. There are trees all along the sides of the road now, their branches mingling over your head. Feel the pebbles of the rough road under your feet.

You are running alone now, for the moment no one is next to you . . . mile after mile, the world is yours . . . you feel strong and in control and you notice there is no breeze now . . . just a stillness and peace as you move smoothly along nearing the 15-mile mark.

The road turns again and your body leans. How does it feel? You can hear footsteps behind you and voices in the quiet. What are they saying . . . what are you saying to yourself as runners begin to catch you? Is there a tightness or fatigue anywhere? Begin to say your affirmations slowly and in rhythm with your stride and breathing. . . . "I am strong." "I feel good."

You run up a small incline, out of the trees, and onto a blacktop road feeling stronger and keeping your form. The wind is at your back and the sun has briefly broken through the clouds. Notice your response to the warmth on your shoulders and the glare from the road. Your legs are still moving smoothly, powerfully . . . thank them . . . thank them for the work they are doing . . . thank them for their strength. Your breathing is even as you approach the final six miles. Someone goes by you with a swoosh . . . you can feel their wind and smell their sweat as they pass and become part of the road moving ahead of you. This is the difficult part of the race . . . the last 10K . . . focus on your form. Notice how strong you are and how your body feels. Say your affirmations again . . . knowing you are close to the end.

You begin to think of your body . . . focusing on your form; you are strong, fit . . . you have trained hard for this race. You thank your legs and body and acknowledge what they have given you. You notice your breathing, taking deep, full breaths . . . visualizing your lungs supplying the rest of your body with oxygen. You begin to push, relaxing your shoulders, keeping a steady pace . . . you notice someone ahead of you and begin to gain on them . . . you come up behind them, passing them quickly . . . picking up the pace for 50 yards and then settling into a comfortable pace. You notice the 23 mile mark . . . only 3.2 miles left. You have covered almost all of it now . . . only a little over a 5K to go . . . a piece of cake! You begin to remember all the 5K races you have run . . . you are passing people now . . . you feel stronger and stronger . . . you remember your word and it fills you with strength, confidence, endurance, and joy . . . a feeling of well-being floods over you . . . you remember some of your affirmations. . . . "I am a strong and powerful runner," . . . "I am smooth and fluid," . . . "My body is fit and fast." . . .

You come to the 25-mile mark and begin to pick up the pace . . . you pass more and more people . . . you are flying in your own world now . . . running, feeling light and free . . . you pass the 26-mile mark . . . you are sprinting now . . . flying . . . feeling the power of victory and accomplishment. . . . The crowds along the course are bigger now . . . there is music . . . are you smiling? The sweat rolls slowly from your eyebrows as you lengthen your stride, passing three runners . . . you can see the finish line banner now as your shoulders relax and you become comfortable with your powerful striding form. Your breath is coming faster and you hear people laughing and shouting. Your feet reach the end . . . the finish line under your shoes . . . you push the button on your watch . . . you have done it! You begin to slow your steps with a deep sigh.

Is there any pain . . . are you floating . . . can you feel your legs at all? Breathe as you walk slowly, looking at the grass now green beneath your shoes . . . hands on your hips. It was a good run . . . a good race . . . you were strong. You remember your affirmations and relax. Someone speaks to you . . . can you remember what they said? Notice the peace surrounding you and your sense of accomplishment. Listen to the music and the announcer as more runners cross the finish line.

The crowds begin to spread out, taking their colors, smells, and sounds with them. You are cooling down . . . your legs relaxing . . . breathing becoming normal . . . what are you saying to yourself?

Become aware of your body now, sitting in the chair or lying on the floor. Feel the contentment as you let go of the picture and slowly come back to your relaxed breathing and the peace and stillnesss. Breathe in . . .

hold it . . . exhale. Say your affirmations and think of your goal. Breathe. . . . When you are ready, open your eyes and reconnect with your present space. Be aware of your body and your breathing. Thank your body for its strength and power, its speed and its health. Give yourself permission to rest, knowing that any time you aim at a goal, you can feel it, see it in your mind's eye, and eventually have it in reality.

GUIDED VISUALIZATION FOR A 100-METER FREESTYLE

(Use the progressive relaxation technique from chap. 4.)

As you focus on your breathing, become aware of the warmth of the room and the smell of the water as you enter the pool area. It is a very familiar smell and feel to your skin. Notice the sounds of the room . . . the echo . . . the water moving . . . the voices . . . you feel right at home and very comfortable. Imagine yourself as you dress down to your suit and begin to stretch and prepare your body to compete. You know this pool . . . it is pretty much like any other pool . . . you move your body . . . stretching . . . bending . . . waiting your turn . . . your name. Be aware of your energy . . . you are well prepared for this race . . . it is your favorite and you are fast and strong . . . you are ready.

You dive into the pool, feeling the water on your skin and hearing the splash as you enter . . . surface and stroke smoothly to the end of the lane. You have always enjoyed warming up . . . moving powerfully and smoothly from one end of the pool to the other . . . gauging your kick turn just right . . . pushing off powerfully and in complete control. You do one more lap and pull yourself up out of the water just as they announce the final call for the 100-meter freestyle. You take your towel . . . drying off just the spots you always dry, and walk to the waiting area . . . you are relaxed and ready . . . you are calm and warm and confident as you walk with the other competitors and stand in front of the block at your designated lane . . . you like this lane. . . .

Become aware of your thoughts and inner focus now as you quiet your body . . . remember your affirmations . . . and that special word or words that connect you with your strength and success. . . . "I am strong and powerful. . . ." "I am a smooth and fast swimmer. . . ." "I am in control and confident. . . ." "I am as good as any other swimmer in the pool today. . . ." You step on the blocks . . . arms easy at your sides . . . breathing deep and full . . . you are ready . . . completely focused and centered . . . you take your mark . . . set . . . and hear the gun. . . .

Your body stretches its full length as you propel yourself off the blocks . . . every muscle extended . . . reaching . . . you feel yourself enter the water . . . cool against your skin . . . you flutter to get as much distance as you can before you surface and begin to stroke . . . you feel powerful and in complete control. You are swimming now . . . stroking easily . . . pulling with great strength and confidence . . . stroke . . . stroke . . . your breathing even and deep . . . every movement efficient and perfect. You are aware that there is someone near you in the next lane . . . you can feel their stroking and hear their splash as you near the end of the pool and ready for your kick turn . . . you put them out of your mind and center yourself for the turn . . . the kick turn is one of your strengths and you lower your head, raising yourself . . . flipping . . . legs over . . . feet against the wall . . . pushing hard . . . in complete control . . . arms outstretched . . . body lengthening . . . reaching . . . cutting smoothly through the water . . . a little flutter and you begin to stroke again. . . .

You feel alone in the pool as you head toward the finish . . . focused completely on your stroking and your breathing . . . you are swimming perfectly . . . doing everything just as it should be done . . . pulling with great force and power . . . kicking perfectly and effectively. As you stroke into the final 25 meters, you sense the swimmer in the next lane again . . . he or she is pushing for the lead . . . you concentrate on your power and dig even deeper with each stroke . . . pulling . . . kicking . . . lowering your head . . . fewer breaths now . . . stroking powerfully . . . reaching . . . pulling . . . surging ahead . . . knowing you can outkick that swimmer . . . any swimmer . . . you are strong and powerful . . . reaching . . . pulling . . . you touch the wall. . . .

You out-touched the next lane . . . you look up for your time . . . it is your best time ever . . . you look down the wall in both directions to see if you have won . . . you have succeeded, and you begin to focus on your breathing. . . . Slowly, you become aware of the noises . . . the colors of the blocks and the timers' clothing . . .

the crowd and other swimmers milling around on the deck above you . . . you are catching your breath . . . feeling the water warm around you . . . you lift yourself out of the pool and stand, reaching for your towel . . . slowing your breath and relaxing into the feelings of excitement and accomplishment . . . you have won . . . you have reached your goal. The feelings rise inside you . . . the pride at having succeeded . . . having given it your best . . . having done well. . . .

Allow yourself to experience it all . . . the congratulations . . . the euphoria . . . the tiredness . . . the joy . . . as you see yourself drying off . . . heading for the area of the room where you left your sweats . . . you feel good . . . it was a good race and you know you did your best . . . you think of your special word or words again . . . it makes you smile. . . .

Begin to come back into your physical space now . . . becoming aware of your breathing . . . deep into your belly . . . hold . . . exhale. Reconnect with your body and the feel of the chair or the floor beneath you. Move your feet and your hands . . . reconnect . . . you are relaxed and rested . . . you are full of new energy and confidence . . . breathe . . . and slowly, when you are ready, open your eyes . . . breathing deeply . . . reconnecting . . . trusting . . . believing in your ability and your strength . . . you are a great swimmer. . . .

Bibliography

Bardwick, J. M., and Douvan, E. *Ambivalence: The socialization of women.* In J. Bardwick (ed.) Readings on the Psychology of Women. New York: Harper and Row, 1972.

Benson, H. *The Relaxation Response.* New York: William Morrow and Co., 1975.

Bernstein, Douglas A. and Borkovec, Thomas D. *Progressive Relaxation Training.* Champaign, Ill.: Research Press, 1973.

Curtis, John and Detert, Richard A. *How to Relax.* Palo Alto, Calif.: Mayfield Publishing Co., 1981.

Davis, Martha, McKay, Mathew, and Eschelman, Elizabeth. *The Relaxation and Stress Reduction Workbook.* Oakland, Calif.: New Harbinger Publications, 1982.

Downing, George. *The Massage Book.* New York: Random House, 1972.

Gallwey, Timothy. *The Inner Game of Tennis.* New York: Random House, 1974.

______ *Inner Skiing,* New York: Random House, 1977.

Garfield, Charles, and Bennett, Hal Zina, *Peak Performance*. Houghton Mifflin Co., 1984.

Gawain, Shakti. *Creative Visualization*. Berkeley, Calif.: Whatever Publishing, 1978.

Griffin, Patricia S. "But She's So Feminine: Changing Mixed Messages We Give To Girls and Women in Sports." *Journal of NAWDAC*, Winter 1984, 9–11.

Hansen, Mark Victor. *Future Diary*. Newport Beach, Calif.: Mark Victor Hansen & Assoc., 1981.

Harris, Dorothy V. and Harris, Bette L. *The Athlete's Guide to Sports Psychology: Mental Skills for Physical People*. New York: Leisure Press, 1984.

Hendricks, Gay and Carlson, J. *The Centered Athlete*. Englewood Cliffs, N.J.: Prentice-Hall, 1982.

Houston, Jean. *The Possible Human*, Los Angeles, Calif.: J. P. Tarcher, 1982.

Jaffe, Dennis T. *Healing from Within*. New York: Knopf, 1980.

Klavora, P. and Daniel, J. ed. *Coach, Athlete, and the Sport Psychologist*. Toronto: University of Toronto Press, 1979.

Laney, Ruth. "Glance Getting Older and Better". *Track & Field News*, May 1985, 25

McCluggage, Denise. *The Centered Skier*. New York: Bantam New Age, 1983.

Mahoney, M. *Self Change: Strategies for Solving Personal Problems*. New York: W. W. Norton & Co., 1979.

Morgan, W.P. "The Mind of the Marathoner," *Psychology Today*, April 1978, 38–49.

Nideffer, R. M. *The Inner Athlete*. New York: Crowell, 1976.

Orlick, Terry. *In Pursuit of Excellence*. Champaign, Ill.: Human Kinetics Publishers, 1980.

Schwarz, Jack. *Voluntary Controls*. New York: Dutton, 1978.

_____ *The Path of Action*. New York: Dutton, 1977.

Spino, Mike. *Breakthrough: Maximum Sports Training*. New York: Pocket Books, 1984.

Suinn, R., ed. *Psychology in Sports: Methods and Applications*. Minneapolis: Burgess Press, 1980.

Syer, John and Connolly, Christopher. *Sporting Body/Sporting Mind*. New York: Cambridge University Press, 1984.

Tutko, Thomas. *Sports Psyching: Playing Your Best Game All of the Time*. Los Angeles: J. P. Tarcher, 1976.

Winter, Bud. *Relax and Win*. La Jolla, Calif.: A. S. Barnes & Co., 1981.

About the Authors

Kay Porter and Judy Foster own Porter Foster, a sports and organizational firm in Eugene, Oregon. Together they have taught mental training techniques to many athletes and teams including the University of Oregon's women's track, tennis, and gymnastics teams, the wrestling team, and the men's and women's swimming teams. Their articles on mental training and the mental processes of such elite athletes as Mary Decker Slaney and Joan Benoit Samuelson have appeared in national magazines.

Kay Porter holds a Ph.D. in Human Developmental Psychology from the University of Oregon, and was a professor at the University of Oregon Center for Gerontology for eight years. She is a masters marathoner.

Judy holds a B.A. in English Literature and Creative Writing from the University of Oregon. She is an artist and an athlete who has taught skiing, swimming, and fiber art in the Pacific Northwest. Judy is a masters sprinter.

Together they conduct clinics, workshops, and seminars on mental training. They have presented their program at the Houston/Tenneco and Boston Marathons, the Olympic Scientific Congress, the Boston Bonne Bell, the Women's Olympic Marathon Trials, the National Masters' Track and Field Championships, the Western Gerontological Society, and the American Medical Jogging Association.

For more information on athletic, business/corporate, and personal seminars, clinics, and workshops, call (503) 342-6875, or write:

PORTER FOSTER, P.O. Box 5584,
Eugene, Oregon, 97405.